D1348779

C014306634

NOT FAR FROM WIGAN PIER

Also available in this series:

Fred Archer	BENEDICT'S POOL
Peter Austen	THE COUNTRY ANTIQUE DEALER
Mary Barnard	THE DIARY OF AN OPTIMIST
Pip Beck	A WAAF IN BOMBER COMMAND
Adrian Bell	THE CHERRY TREE
Mary Sydney Burke	THE SOLDIER'S WIFE
Jennifer Davies	TALES OF THE OLD GYPSIES
Roger Hutchings	CRYSTAL PALACE VISTAS
Ken Hankins	A CHILD OF THE THIRTIES
Herbert C. Harrison	THE MILL HOUSE AND THEREABOUTS
Gregory Holyoake	THE PREFAB KID
Erma Harvey James	WITH MAGIC IN MY EYES
Joy Lakeman	THEM DAYS
Len Langrick	SNOWBALL: GO FIND YOURSELF A SCHOOL
Florence Mary McDowell	OTHER DAYS AROUND ME
Madeline MacDonald	THE LAST YEAR OF THE GANG
Angela Mack	DANCING ON THE WAVES
Brian P. Martin	TALES FROM THE COUNTRY PUB
Roger Mason	GRANNY'S VILLAGE
Cicely Mayhew	BEADS ON A STRING
Christian Miller	A CHILDHOOD IN SCOTLAND
Katharine Moore	QUEEN VICTORIA IS VERY ILL
J. C. Morten	I REMAIN, YOUR SON JACK
and Sheila Morten	
Pauline Neville	PEGGY
Humphrey Phelps	JUST ACROSS THE FIELDS
Angela Raby	THE FORGOTTEN SERVICE
Phyl Surman	PRIDE OF THE MORNING
Doreen Louie West	LOUIE: AN OXFORD LADY
Elizabeth West	HOVEL IN THE HILLS
Hazel Wheeler	HALF A POUND OF TUPPENNY RICE
William Woodrow	ANOTHER TIME, ANOTHER PLACE

Not Far From Wigan Pier

*Nostalgic Short Stories of Lancashire
(Revised Edition)*

Ted Dakin

ISIS
LARGE PRINT
Oxford and Orlando

Copyright © Edward Dakin, 1999

First published in Great Britain 1999
by Horseshoe Publications

Published in Large Print 2001 by ISIS Publishing Ltd,
7 Centremead, Osney Mead, Oxford OX2 0ES
by arrangement with Horseshoe Publications

British Library Cataloguing in Publication Data
Dakin, Ted
   Not far from Wigan pier. – Large print ed. –
   (Isis reminiscence series)
   1. Large type books 2. Lancashire (England) – Social life and
   customs – 20th century – Fiction
   I. Title
   823.9'14[F]

ISBN 0-7531-6479-5 (hb)
ISBN 0-7531-6480-9 (pb)

Printed and bound by Antony Rowe, Chippenham and Reading

CONTENTS

Black Gold

Mayflower Road in the nineteen-thirties was landlord owned and slummy. It was a sub-district of Wigan, a cotton town in the heart of Lancashire. I was born in Mayflower Road, at number twenty-six, and Lonnie lived next door at twenty-four. Our road was a cobbled one, but once past the property it changed drastically, becoming rugged and pot-holed and led to a canal footpath, and into the countryside.

We were like brothers, Lonnie and me. Inseparable. Same school, same church, same likes and dislikes. And after leaving school, same problem; no work. So we turned to crime. Our first criminal act was stealing timber. If it was get-at-able, we would take it. Once removed from it's rightful owner we would reduce it to small pieces and sell it off as kindling wood.

But we weren't satisfied. The greed for more money was strong within us. We decided to move on to something more lucrative. Coal. Shimmering and shiny, Black Gold.

* * *

The geography of our beggarly district was simple. To the west a canal. To the east a railway track, and sandwiched between, Mayflower Road. By the tracks, on nearby sidings, tons of coal were piled high into tantalising, miniature mountains. It had been mined from local pits and dumped there to await collection and transportation to various parts of the country. The coal was there, and Lonnie and me, like many of our kind, couldn't resist the temptation. We stole it and sold it for one shilling and sixpence a bag. But it wasn't easy. Stealing the coal was hard and dangerous work, and there was fierce competition. Our many rivals were both cunning and fearless. Competition, such as it was, worried Lonnie and me and prompted us to reconsider our uncertain future. How could two seventeen year olds compete with men of experience, strength and guile? Then one day the Goddess of Fate stepped in.

* * *

It was a hot and humid day, and as was their wont on such days, the tenants of Mayflower Road stood in groups gossiping about everything and nothing. Lonnie and me were squatting against Mrs. Leeter's gable-end pitching pebbles at a battered tin can. A shadow fell across the pavement.

"Morning boys."

We jumped to our feet. It was Father Dillon, our Parish priest.

"Morning, Father," we chorused.

His tall, spare figure seemed even taller and leaner. The sun, now at it's zenith, highlighted the frayed cuffs and the shine of his clerical black, and glinted on rimless glasses, behind which, blue, quick and intelligent eyes missed nothing.

"Still no work then, boys?"

His very presence disturbed everyone. Most of the locals had already vanished indoors. His sermonising and waif and stray collections were so notorious that everyone avoided him. All Catholics (even the Pope too, some said) feared him.

"Been to mass lately?"

Lonnie beat me to it.

"Last Sunday, Father."

"And what about confession?"

Keen blue eyes scrutinised our every fidget and shuffle. I took a deep breath. It was my turn to lie.

"My Mam's been ill, Father — I've been busy running errands — and things."

"Hmm, poor soul, I hope she's improving. Well, how do you pass the time, boys, that is apart from running errands — and things?"

"Looking for work, Father," Lonnie said.

"Not sinful work, I hope."

He took out a packet of Woodbines, appeared to count them, selected one and put a match to it.

"You won't be helping yourselves to — what do they call it — to any Black Gold, will you now?"

"No Father," I said, "we've heard about it, but that's about all." He didn't seem to be listening.

"No matter," he said, "soon, very soon, the coal, the Black Gold, the temptation, will be gone — and about time too."

Lonnie gave me a worried glance, coughed, and said:

"How's that again, Father? Did you say the coal is to go?"

"Transportation begins on Sunday, boys, by this time next week there won't be one solitary nugget left to steal. And about time too," he said again.

* * *

Later that day we talked about Father Dillon. We were convinced that the priest had something to do with the coal's removal.

"He thinks he's God," Lonnie said.

"Perhaps he is, in disguise," I said.

The following day Lonnie told me about an idea he'd had. He called it his Master Plan, and was quite excited. It was to be a final foray before our only means of income disappeared for ever. For Lonnie's plan to work we made a crude but sturdy raft, collected a few extra sacks, did some furtive reconnaissance, and waited nervously for Sunday to come round.

* * *

On that chosen Sabbath, Lonnie and I set off early. This was to be our final — and we hoped — our most profitable foray. A fine drizzle fell bringing with it a shroud of mist. As we scrambled through the perimeter fence I could hear the faint peal of St. Joseph's ancient bell. Once inside the fence we crawled in long drenched grass until we reached the limits of cover. Lonnie, who was leading the way, cautioned for extra care. We hadn't long to wait. The heavy labouring sounds of a locomotive grew louder by the second. A panic attack turned my stomach into a cage of struggling butterflies. I felt sick. Parting the grass we could see, lumbering towards us out of the mist, the massive clanking engine. Several jolting wagons, each one piled high with precious coal, followed in tow.

Our plan was simple. As the train drew level we would board one of the wagons, fill several sacks with coal and throw them over the side. By this time, the slow-moving train would be opposite Bulrush Pool, a stagnant pond, which formed part of the railway's boundary, and where our raft lay concealed. Collection and transportation across the pool would be the easiest part of the operation.

Suddenly, the engine, struggling and belching steam, drew level. Lonnie gave my sleeve a sharp tug, took a firmer grip of his sacks, and sprinted across the clearing. With choking heartbeats, I followed. Lonnie, with the agility of an acrobat, boarded the last wagon. I did likewise, almost losing my footing on the greasy bodywork, and fell gasping for breath beside him. We set to work. We had to move fast. Without tying it, we threw the first bag over the side. Coal spewed out into the tall grass. The engine slowed down causing the wagons to jolt together. That would be the first bend. We crouched low, feverishly filling the next sack. Then a third. With hands black and bleeding, we slaved on. Another jolting and juddering, followed by the deafening squeal of brakes, played havoc with my nerves. Time was running out. As we threw the last sack overboard Lonnie gave the thumbs up sign. Over the edge we clambered, clinging for dear life to the slippery bodywork. Lonnie looked back, gave me one of his impish grins, and began to inch his way towards the buffers. As he reached the corner of the wagon there was a fearful lurch as several sets of buffers bounced together. Lonnie, struggling to keep his balance, lost his footing and slipped from sight. I yelled out his name, then jumped. I landed heavily and slid out of control down a steep grassy slope. A painful, head-on collision with something hard brought me to an agonising stop. The last thing I heard before blacking-out, was the loud and piercing shriek of the train's whistle.

* * *

When Adolf Hitler marched into Poland, Lonnie was still in hospital. His right leg had been amputated below the knee and there were still complications with his other one. I couldn't bring myself to visit him. To see Lonnie's broken body would have destroyed me. There was inside me a gnawing guilt, a guilt that brought on fits of deep depression and nightmares. However, one day the cure for this malady arrived in the form of an official brown envelope. The King's army beckoned. The war that had seemed so remote was now only a troop-ship away.

While at training camp I received my first letter from Lonnie. It was newsy and humorous. He ended the letter with a postscript.

By the way — it read — I've had numerous visits from our friend, Father Dillon, and he's almost persuaded me to take the vows and enter the church. Can you imagine it, Eric, me a priest, and a one-legged one at that? I never saw Lonnie again.

* * *

Before going overseas, myself and a few thousand more were given forty-eight hour passes.

Mam was tearful for the whole two days, and Dad, who had done his bit in the First World War, wanted to take me out on the town. Naturally, I made my excuses and spent time doing my own thing, teaming up with old mates, visiting relatives, then indulging in a soldier's favourite pastime. Booze, Woodbines and girls! Simple, enjoyable, and bodily satisfying. Things that were essential to someone who may never again see the shores of England.

My final night was a humdinger, and I woke with a throbbing head. I took a walk to ease the pain. I wandered by the canal and stopped on Elston Bridge. I gazed eastwards towards Mayflower Road. Over the rooftops I could see something that I thought had gone forever. Silhouetted against the skyline stood great piles of coal. It was back again. The nuggets were blok, shining in the afternoon sun. Just like Black Gold.

Nothing Lasts Forever

"Nothing lasts forever," my Dad used to say. "Time changes all things and everybody."

I used to look at him and wonder what the hell he was going on about. But it wasn't long before I found out.

My school was a catholic school with a reputation for winning rugby matches, so if you attended church on a regular basis and played rugby, you were accepted as a model pupil.

The "college" as it was jokingly called, was Dickensian in character and just a spit away from Wigan Pier. It was attended by a multitude of snotty nose roughnecks, who, out of school hours aggravated the already atrocious conditions by attacking the buildings and breaking as many windows as possible.

In harmony with this miserable establishment, the teachers, especially the headmaster, were strict disciplinarians who used various forms of punishment to curb our general wildness. The school didn't possess a flagged or macadamed playground, ours was called the "broo", an undulating brick and glass littered patch of land, where playtime was more risky than trekking across the Andes in a snow storm.

Owd Hector, the headmaster, was the most feared of all the teachers. His word was law. And his word was

enforced by a shiny, wicked looking cane. Some said
that his methods of punishment had been copied by the
Gestapo! Owd Hector's wish was to have the best and
most consistent rugby team in the whole of the school
league. Consequently, teaching unruly kids came second
on his list of priorities. He was so keen on the game that
a piece of land adjacent to the "broo" was used for team
training and tactics. He had even appointed a rugby
coach, a Mr Nelson, who was an ex-army officer. Mr
Nelson's sole purpose was to teach rugby football and
by any means he thought necessary.

* * *

That particular year, Mr Nelson's team was doing well
and another inscribed silver cup in the bulging trophy
case was almost a certainty.

Then disaster struck. The team's right winger and top
try scorer was knocked down by a car and badly injured.
Owd Hector was in a tizzy; within hours he was on the
prowl for new talent. He wanted another ace winger and
the hunt was on. Boys were chosen at random and I was
one of them.

Trial games were played, with Hector and Mr Nelson
watching each newcomer with eagle-eyed scrutiny. My
turn came one wet and windy afternoon. Funnily enough
I played well. Perhaps it was because I wasn't trying.
My sport was boxing, and nobody, not Nelson, not even
Hector would ever push me into something I didn't want
to do. Boxing was my life. Nothing else mattered.
Anyway, it was far more desirous to meet one opponent

inside a neat square than attempt to stop a pack of glory hunting dervishes on a mucky football field.

However, the damage was done, and I had been chosen, if Hector put a claim on someone that was it. Excuses weren't accepted. But I was stubborn and resentful. I had every intention of doing my worst. A couple of days later my chance came. It was now or never. As prearranged I was playing on the wing. Every time the ball came my way I would feign cramp and roll over on the ground grunting and groaning and clutching my leg, or foot. After the game, Mr Nelson was furious and threatening.

"Those were deliberate cock-ups, laddie," he raved.

I protested my innocence and promised to do better next time. He gave me a murderous look and said:

"You had better, laddie, or I march you in front of the headmaster, the choice is yours."

Knowing the reputation of our sadistic, trophy hunting headmaster, I decided to abandon all pretences. It now seemed more sensible to face thirteen potential limb-breakers on a rugby field than face Hector in his study. Gone were my aspirations to be a pugilistic world champion.

In the following game I scored three tries. Then, lo and behold, it happened again. I couldn't help it. I was a natural. Slowly but surely the transition began. I was fitter and tougher than I had ever been, and the amazing thing was I was enjoying myself. What made the game so special was the adulation. After scoring some fantastic try I would be swamped by mud-caked, sweating and appreciative team-mates, and believe me the feeling was euphoric. Then came the fans, especially the girls. I'd never known anything like it. There were never girls at boxing matches; but out there in the cold and wet, muffled and bonneted, they would scream like mad, prompting and urging as though it was the last game in the world. And later, out on the streets, they would give me the "glad eye" and stop and talk, hinting and posing, and chattering loads of rubbish. But it was good rubbish. Very good rubbish.

This rugby game had turned out better than I had ever dreamed. We became invincible. Nothing or no one could stop us. Side after side fell to our prowess. By this time I wanted that cup more than Owd Hector. At last the big event drew near, in two days time we were due to meet St. John's. This was it. Everybody was raring to go.

On the day of the match I was woken by Mother.

"Come on love, the big day is here, rise and shine." I couldn't answer. I was gagging and swallowing painfully.

"What's the matter, lad?" Mother said.

"It's mi throat," I whispered. She took a closer look, peering into my mouth.

"There's no Cup Final for you, my lad. You've got tonsillitis."

That day, lying there with the sound of rain lashing against the bedroom window, I prayed fervently for every team member.

"Please, God," I whispered, "please help them to win this match, because if they don't, Owd Hector will skin me alive."

It must have been God's day off. My prayers went unanswered and we lost fourteen points to nil.

Innocent, yet convicted I returned to school. Judge and jury were poised. The punishment began. I was ridiculed and spurned. Fans (including the girls) deserted me. Then came the bombshell. With ruthless execution I was booted off the team. I was devastated. Then came the final humiliation. It was time to face Owd Hector.

I stood trembling before him. He rose from his chair and walked slowly to the front of his desk. He held his cane like a rifle, resting it against his right shoulder. I gulped and took a step back. He smiled.

"Where've you been, laddie?"

"Sick, Sir."

"Sick?" He seemed to savour the word.

"Ill, Sir. My Mam sent you a note, Sir."

"A note?"

"To say I was sick, Sir. She sent it in with Bobby Smith from standard six, Sir."

"Bobby Smith? Never heard of him."

"But . . ."

"Bend over, laddie."

And with every swish of Hector's cane I clenched my teeth and thought of Dad and his words of wisdom.

Nothing lasts forever . . . Nothing lasts forever . . . Nothing lasts forever.

The Bones of the Dead

I looked back and saw Grandad, hand on tiller, framed against a dying sun, looking for all the world like a figure of doom. Ahead, in the oncoming twilight, I could see the familiar dark and looming mills of Wigan. I sighed and gave Jenny's bridle a gentle tug.

"We won't be long, girl, we'll soon be home."

The mare, sensing my mood, shook her head and snorted, sending clouds of vapour into the cold, clear air.

Grandad was a boatman, who, for some forty-odd years had made a living from hiring out his boat, to carry anything, from coal to cotton, from anyplace to anywhere. Now, the hiring was over. We had made our last delivery. The Zulu and Jenny were up for sale, which left our future prospects looking somewhat bleak.

* * *

Years earlier the trading of cotton and coal had relied heavily on the many local waterways, which had prompted Grandad to take a gamble. Within weeks he had become the proud owner of a horse-drawn canal boat and a house and stable, not far from Wigan Pier. Cotton from the mills, and coal from the surrounding pits, and Grandad was in the big time.

For years all went well. Then disaster struck. The first setback came in the guise of steel tracks. All too soon, mile upon mile of metal rails scarred the countryside. The steam train took over. The age of speed had arrived. Slowly, but relentlessly, the canal trade began to dwindle, and Grandad's business went into slow decline.

The second clout was delivered by Aunt Clara, Grandad's only daughter. She was married to an Irish waffler called Pat, who had a weakness for taking risks. As most gamblers do, Pat fell into debt, and owed money to everyone but the Pope, which left Pat with only one alternative, a moonlight flit back to his homeland. However, soon fed up with an over abundance of Guinness, spuds, and priests, Aunt Clara — now pregnant — yearned for home. Her letters, blotched by many tears, pleaded with her father to bring her, and her unborn child back to England. Already teetering on the brink, those pitiful letters gave Grandad the final push. His decision was all consuming; sell the Zulu and Jenny, pay off Pat's outstanding debts and ship the family back home.

Once through Paxton Locks, the smoking stacks of our neighbourhood came into view. A few minutes later, with the Zulu moored and Jenny unhitched, we led her from the canal bank towards home. The path took us past Jack Calman's factory — known locally as the boneyard — whose wordy sign announced to all and sundry that: J. J. CALMAN & SON, SUPPLIED SELECTED HIDES, THE FINEST GLUES, AND GENUINE BONE-MEAL FERTILIZER.

We hurried on, trying in vain not to inhale the unholy stench which was a permanent reminder of their produce. As we went along, a rickety wagon piled high with bones of many slaughtered beast, rumbled past. "The bones of the dead," Grandad said solemnly.

We crossed Gambler's field which linked Calman's factory to the very cobbles of our ancient borough. At the corner, where snot-nosed kids played under the gas lamp, we parted company.

The following Sunday, tea over and done, Mam knitting and Dad round at Grandad's, we had a visitor. It was Father Dillon, the parish priest. The purpose of these between-mass visits, was twofold. One; to catch as many lapse Catholics as possible and to give them a sermon. And two; to collect as much money as possible for the church and for the town's waifs and strays.

With another sixpence secured inside his blue money bag, Father Dillon settled down in Dad's armchair. Apart from his work as a cleric the priest also enjoyed a Sunday diet of tea, biscuits and tasty gossip.

"Well, young Eric, how's life down on the canal?"

He smiled broadly.

"What a life, eh, plenty of fresh air and honest to goodness toil, what more can a man ask for?"

"There'll be no more toil. Father," Mam said, "it's over and done with; Grandad's selling up."

"Well I'm amazed. Dear me. Poor souls. You must be devastated."

"Which brings us to the question of money, Father."

The priest nibbled a biscuit and sipped some tea.

"Money?"

"Aye, money," replied Mam. "There'll be none for the church now. We'll need every penny."

"Dear, dear. Ah well, as Mr Micawber once said, 'Something will turn up.'" Mam sniffed.

"I hope he's right . . . where does he work this Mr Thingummy . . . he might find our Eric a job."

The priest caught my eye and smiled.

"I don't know about Mr Micawber but I know someone who just might . . . Do you know a Mr Kyle, Eric?"

"You mean Amos Kyle, the rat-catcher?"

"That's the chap . . . well I do believe he's on the lookout for an assistant but seems to be having problems."

No bloody wonder, I thought.

"Eric would be ever so grateful," Mam said. "Wouldn't you, Eric?"

"He's probably found somebody by now," I said hopefully.

"No, no, I don't think so," Father Dillon said.

He eased himself out of Dad's chair and with three long, urgent strides, he was stood at the door.

"No, no, I'm quite sure the job's still open . . . Tell you what, I'll have a word and get him to call round . . . how about that?"

And before this could be confirmed or denied, he lifted the latch and was gone.

True to his word, Father Dillon had Amos Kyle call round, and I soon realized that any agreement on my part was quite unnecessary. Our wily priest had seen to that. He had no intentions of missing any of our weekly donations. Not even one.

Mam gave Amos a wedge of home-made cake and a mug of tea. Dinky, his battle-scarred mongrel, was taken through to the back yard and given a dish of water. Amos, the only ratter for miles around, was scruffy and unschooled, but possessed an inbuilt craftiness that surfaced as intelligence. His present employer was Jack Calman. Apparently Jack always demanded immediate action, which wasn't surprising. Bonemeal, which Jack sold in bulk as crop fertilizer, was made from powdered animal bone and was the firm's main produce. Rats loved the stuff and thrived on it. It was Amos's professionalism that gave substance to Jack's personal motto: "Kill the rats and feed the crops."

Between bites of cake and slurps of tea the ratter gave me a brief outline of what was to be my first ratting expedition.

"We'll start tonight," Amos said.

"Tonight? But it's Friday."

"Aye, but it'll give us all weekend to collect our tails."

"Tails?"

"Aye, tails. That's how Jack Calman pays me; a bob a tail."

"A shilling? That's not much."

"It is if you catch enough."

"What's your average then?"

"In one night? . . . Let me see . . . I've bagged as many as forty . . . happen fifty on a good night."

"That many?"

"Aye, an' Jack Calman's no fool, he wants proof o' puddin', so to speak, so I gives him the tails to shut him up."

As if to give credence to this infallible method, he tapped his head with a grimy forefinger and winked.

At twelve that night, armed to the teeth with clubs and traps, and Amos Kyle's patent rat poison, we made our way to Calman's factory. As we crossed over the muddy yard, Amos briefed me once again as to his proven methods. Dinky's job was to flush out and kill as many rats as possible. The ones lucky enough to escape his savage fangs would fall victim to our clubs. Once the physical onslaught was over, traps would be set and poison pushed down the many infested tunnels that ran under and around the premises. The poison, inducing tremendous thirst, would force the rats to the surface where they would die an agonising death. The next day, the tails would be lopped and added to the rest.

At the door of an half-timbered warehouse, Amos whispered his final instructions.

"The dog goes in first, then you. I'll switch on the lights . . . you go left, I go right . . . Right?"

"I think so, but what do I do next?"

"Bloody hell! I've told you once. You see a rat, you club the bugger . . . Right?"

"Right."

Slowly, without a sound, he opened the door. Dinky, needing no command, bounded off into the darkness. Heart pounding out of control, I followed. In the sudden glare of light I froze solid. Dinky was nowhere to be seen . . . Amos already on the run and club at the ready, flung out an arm.

"Down there!" he shouted. "Left! Left!"

The fertilizer, ready and bagged, was stacked into neat, regimented rows. I ran down a narrow alleyway and skidded to a stop. In front of me, dozens of the devils were feeding on meal that had spewed from rat gnawed sacks. Rooted to the spot, I waved my club timidly. Suddenly, Dinky, his muzzle already smeared with blood, bounced into view. The rats, trapped between us and sensing death, took the better option and scurried towards me. Hump-backed and squeaking like mad, they closed in. I was petrified. One ran over my foot. Dinky bit into it, shook it and then pounced on another. Galvanised into action, I struck out and missed. I struck again, strongly, accurately. A kind of madness overcame me. Skulls cracked, and bodies pulped under my lethal club. Between the dog and me, the dead lay strewn, like some bizarre field of battle. And so it went on; the clubbing, the kicking, the savaging. I was acting way out of character, but the power of life and death over this scurrying vermin was stimulating and euphoric.

Eventually, the slaughter stopped. Survivors escaped the best way they could. Some ran overhead, along rusting girders and roof supports to vanish into nooks and crannies. Exhausted but triumphant, we collected the dead. Outside, by torchlight, we set traps and laid poison. My first night's work was over. It was time to go home.

* * *

Grandad was having problems. He couldn't sell either the Zulu or Jenny, and Aunt Clara was still in Ireland. Still writing letters. As time went on, Grandad's good

19

intentions began to weaken. In a futile attempt to bolster his flagging determination he turned to drink. To buy drink he would sell anything. Resolutions were now a thing of the past.

A few weeks after my first ratting experience, Grandad came calling. His knocking was loud and continuous and on opening the front door it was quite obvious to me that the old man was very drunk. He was holding on grimly to Jenny's bridle.

"I'm glad you're in, lad," he slurred. "I've made a sale, I've sold Jenny."

"That's good, Grandad, good. Who's she goin' to?"

"Will you come wi' me, lad? Just for company, like."

"Course I will, wait a minute, I'll get mi jacket."

Mam was still at the table sipping tea.

"I wouldn't go if I was you, Eric."

"I think I'd better, Mam, by the looks of Grandad he could do with some help."

"Don't go, Eric, you won't like it."

"None of us wants to see Jenny go, Mam, but Grandad needs the cash. You know that."

"It's blood money, Eric, that's what it is."

"What are you going on about, Mam?"

"He's sold her to Timpson's, lad, not far from Wigan Pier. She's being sold as horse meat. He's having her slaughtered."

"God Almighty! He wouldn't do that, not Grandad . . . never."

"It's the only sale he could make, Eric. Leave him to it. Let him do his own dirty work."

I went to the door. Grandad, keen to be off, began to shout again. "C'mon, lad, what you waiting for? C'mon, let's be off."

"You lied to me, Grandad."

"What you goin' on about? I've never lied to you . . . never."

"You lied about Jenny, about making a sale."

"I didn't lie. I've sold her I tell you."

"Aye, to Timpson's. What kind o' sale is that, eh?"

The old man's eyes began to fill up. He patted the mare fondly and said:

"It's the only way, Eric, lad. I've tried me best but nobody wants her, or the damn boat . . . that's goin' too, I'm burning it."

"I'm sorry, Grandad, I can't come with you. It doesn't seem right."

"C'mon, lad, keep me company. I'm only leaving her, you won't see owt."

"I'll go as far as Wigan Pier, then you're on your own, alright?"

Twenty minutes later I was back home. The short journey had been a sorry affair with Grandad giving voice to his convictions that he was doing the right thing.

Mother had company. Amos Kyle, who was doing justice once again to Mam's home made baking, welcomed me with enthusiasm.

"Ere's me mate. Where 'ave you bin, Eric, and wot's up wi' thi face?"

Mam caught my look, put a finger to her pursed lips and shook her head.

"I'm alright, Amos. What brings you round here?"

"Well, I've come to cheer thi up."

"Oh, aye."

"Aye, but there's a bit o' bad goes wi' it."

"Have another piece of cake, Amos," Mam said.

Helping himself from an already depleted plate, Amos said:

"Jack Calman wants to see us, Eric. He wants to pay us up."

"That's quick," I said. "It's only bin six weeks."

Devouring the last of his cake, Amos spread his hands, examined his grimy fingernails and winked.

"When your as good as us, Eric . . . The draw back is of course, we're now out of work."

"You'll be alright, Amos," Mam said, "there's still plenty folk bothered wi' rats."

"That's so, but they don't pay as much as Jack Calman, not by a long chalk."

He drained his cup.

"C'mon, Eric, Jack Calman'll think wiv getten lost."

We had just reached the factory gates when Jack Calman's car drew up. He sounded his horn, got out, and came across to us.

"Amos, Eric, I thought I'd missed you."

"Not likely, Mr Calman," Amos said, "not when there's money involved." Taking the hint, Jack took out his wallet and began counting notes into Amos's outstretched hand.

"And there's your bonus," he said, "and here's another fiver for not wasting time . . . Thanks Amos, the pair of you have done brilliant."

"You're a toff, Mr Calman," Amos said.

"Aye, thanks," I said. "We never expected that much, Mr Calman."

"I can afford it, Eric . . . What's our motto, Amos?"

"Er . . ."

"Kill the rats and feed the crops, that's my motto, Eric."

"Aye, that's it," Amos said.

"And the more crops I feed the more money I make — my only trouble is keeping up with demand."

"That should be easy enough," Amos said.

"It would be with another lorry or two . . . I've enough fertilizer to cover half of England and not enough transport to get shut."

"Expensive things is lorries," Amos said.

"I'll say."

"It'll be cheaper hirin' a boat," Amos said.

"A canal boat? I've never thought about it. Anyway, there's not many about these days."

"No problem there, is there Eric?"

I kicked a stone and did some nervous shuffling. God! What a fix to be in.

"Him and his Grandad'll do as many deliveries as you like, won't you, Eric?"

"You mean bring the old man out of retirement?"

"That's it. He'll jump at the chance, won't he Eric? And he'll deliver direct; there's many a farm close to t'cut."

"It's slow by boat," Jack Calman said.

"But a boat can carry more than a lorry."

"That's true . . . Hmmm, how about it, Eric?"

"It's no use," I said, "it's too late."

"What the hell you goin' on about, Eric?" Amos said.
"Too late for what?"

"It's Grandad, he's gone and sold Jenny . . . She's gone . . ."

"Sold her? Who to? When?"

"She's been put down," I said.

"Put down? . . . You mean . . . ?"

"I mean killed. Slaughtered . . . slaughtered and sold for horse meat."

"Bloody hell!" Amos said.

"I'm sorry, Eric," Jack Calman said, "the old man must be out of his mind."

"That's for sure," Amos said.

"You don't understand, Mr Calman . . . he had to do it . . . there was no other way . . . anyway, it's over an' done wi'."

"I'm really sorry, Eric," Jack said.

"I'll be gettin' on home now," I said. "Thanks again for the money."

I left Amos and Jack still talking and made my way back home. On reaching home I was surprised to see Grandad sitting on the doorstep.

"What you doin' here, Grandad? Why don't you go in?"

"Waiting o'you, Eric. Where've you bin?"

"Collect me wages from Jack Calman."

"It's good to have a jingle in thi pocket."

"Money's not everything, Grandad."

"It is when tha short of it."

"It's funny how things go, isn't it," I said.

"Go on, tell me, lad."

24

"An hour ago wi had nowt, now wiv gotten' money to chuck away."

"Speak for the sel', lad, I've gotten' nowt."

"Surely it's not gone to the Three Crowns already."

"Nay, lad, I've nowt to spend on ale, or owt else for that matter."

"Are they makin' you wait then?"

"There'll be no money comin' to me, Eric."

"I don't understand, I thought you'd done a deal?"

"I couldn't go through wi' it, lad. When tha left mi near Wigan Pier, Jenny began to act up."

"What do you mean?"

"Like she does when we're off on a trip . . . Know what I mean?"

"She'd got a whiff of the cut," I said.

Grandad smiled.

"Anyroad, she's back in her stable waitin' for a miracle."

"Do you believe in miracles, Grandad?"

"I've never seen one yet."

"Then hang on to your braces," I said.

And I began running back towards Calman's factory as fast as I could.

An Unforgettable Christmas

When you come to think, most Christmases are mediocre affairs, and are soon forgotten. But some are unforgettable and stay with you for life. Every so often, especially when Christmas comes around, they surface and make you wish once again for the happy times you once knew. You may think my recollections of one particular Christmas a bit odd, but this is how it was.

* * *

It was Christmas Eve, and Dad had nipped out for a couple of gills, so our Mam, hoping to grab five minutes peace, wrapped two hot oven shelves inside two owd pullovers and ushered me and our kid off to bed. On a bitterly cold night there was nowt nicer than diving into bed with two hot oven shelves and our kid. It were champion.

We lay there for ages, me and our kid, talking about the presents we wanted most. I wanted a mouth-organ. I couldn't play one, but our kid, who had got one the Christmas before, had promised to show me. Eventually we talked ourselves out and went to sleep.

Have you ever put your bare foot on a red hot oven shelf? I don't recommend it, but it is definitely the best alarm clock known to man. To avoid this painful experience, take an ample square of good quality blanket — not a tattered owd pullover like Mam did — wrap the shelf securely, and hope for the best. Anyhow, once awake I wanted a pee. Not wanting to waken our kid, I slid out of bed and began searching for the po. I couldn't find it. I tried again. Where was that soddin' po? For the second time that night I cursed Mam rotten. I didn't fancy one bit the fifteen yard sprint to the outside lavvy; but it had to be done. As Confucius once said: "When humble man got to go, humble man got to go." Or something like that. I hopped gingerly across the cold linoleum and down the stairs. Just as I reached the back door I heard voices. Mam and Dad were still up. Dad sounded happy.

"Well, love, is everything ready?"

"I hope so," Mam said.

Dad laughed.

"I can't wait to see their faces."

"Me neither," Mam said. "I hope they're both satisfied."

"They're not daft, they know we haven't much money."

"It's Christmas," Mam said. "Kids don't bother about money, all they think about is presents."

"I thought once about selling young Walter," Dad said.

"Now just a minute," Mam said, "Mam and Dad gave us Walter knowing full well he'd have a good home. They'd never forgive us."

I shivered and crossed my legs again. Young Walter had become a family joke. Actually, it was a painting by Millais, called "Boyhood of Raleigh" and shows a young Walter Raleigh sat on a rocky shore with an "old sea dog" staring wistfully out to sea. The picture took pride of place over our mantelpiece and to lose it would have been like a family bereavement.

"It was only a thought . . . I was only thinking of the kids," Dad said.

"I know, love, but you know what they're like, the more they get the more they want."

"Well, they'll have to want. You can't get much on dole money."

"I hope they're satisfied," Mam said.

"They'll be satisfied," Dad said confidently, "especially our Eric, he's no mard sod."

I felt right proud. I never realised that Dad thought that about me.

"By the way," Mam said, "did you get that mouth-organ down from the top shelf?"

"'Eck, no. It's a good job you reminded me."

That was enough for me. As long as I was getting that mouth-organ I didn't give tuppence. I let myself out into the freezing night and was so excited I had a pee in the grid.

* * *

I tried to act casual on that Christmas morning, but soon gave up. How can you act casual when you've waited forever for something you really want? So, like all kids do on that very special day we both made a dive for our respective parcels. It was all over in a flash. The hurried tearing of paper. The searching. The disappointment. A torch. A writing set. That was it! I couldn't believe it. Where was the mouth-organ I so dearly wanted? I looked at Dad looking at me. He smiled. Was this some joke? Was he having me on? It must be in the stocking hanging from the mantelpiece. With shaking hands I emptied the contents. Everything was edible. Chocolate. Nuts. Chewing gum. Fruit. Then came the killer blow. From behind me came the harmonious notes of the thing I wanted most. I fought back the tears.

"What's the matter, lad?" Dad said. "Aren't tha pleased?"

I looked at my brother, eyes bright with emotion, sucking and blowing the tunes I knew, but couldn't play. Then I remembered what Dad had said to Mam just a few hours earlier.

"Just what I wanted, Dad," I said. "Thanks."

That night, after tea, our kid's harmonious renderings nearly brought the house down. And Dad's singing too made the gas mantle shiver and shake in its holder. All too soon it came to an end. Mam decided to call time, and Dad, slightly huffed raised his glass of stout, and quoting from one of his many well read books, said in a loud voice.

"And as Tiny Tim once said, 'God Bless us Every one'."

And Mam, slightly tipsy on too much cooking sherry, raised her glass as well, and looking up at the family heirloom, said with a giggle:

"And a Merry Christmas to you too, young Walter."

Whereupon, Young Walter, not to be out-done by the noise of mere mortals, left his long-time perch, and crashed to the floor in a shower of glass.

Pegleg's Prize

It was rabbits in a pet shop window that triggered my memory. How time goes. It seemed like only yesterday. I remember it distinctly.

It was Saturday morning and my Mam was shaking me, waking me up in that rough way she had. For one horrible moment I thought it was Monday morning. Then through the fog, came her voice, clear, urgent, compelling.

"Eric! Eric! C'mon, your Uncle Albert from Liverpool is here."

That did it. From the bed I shot like a bullet from a pistol, and down the stairs two at a time before my Mam could even draw breath. Reason? Simple! With every visit, Uncle Albert brought me a present, and to a kid of twelve that was the best reason in the world. This time it was a rabbit. A shivering, doe-eyed ball of fur. I called it Dobbin, and Dad knocked together a simple hutch made from orange boxes.

Everything went well for a few months. Each day after school I would hurry home, free Dobbin from his hutch and keep a look out for prowling cats while he had a hop round the yard.

Then, quite suddenly it came to a stop. I lost interest. As my Dad used to say: "Nothing lasts forever." He was a great philosopher was my Dad. Anyway, this is what happened. Mam had sent me for our usual Friday kippers from the corner shop, when I saw this vision. It was Birdy Briggs, flashing past in a whirl of exotic colours and gleaming chrome. I stood there mesmerised. How could he afford a bike like that? And where did he get it from? Later, I found out. His Dad, who worked down the pit, was paying Knocker Neill, a neighbour of ours, two bob a week until it was paid off. Knocker, was an odd character who made a living collecting old bike frames and the necessary spare parts. Then, with meticulous care, spent hour after hour repairing and cleaning them. Finally he would assemble them into roadworthy machines and finish them off with a few deft strokes of enamel paint. Naturally, like all greedy kids, I wanted a Knocker Neill bike of my own, but I couldn't have one, could I? Dad was on the dole and the cash Mam made from taking in washing was spent to keep us fed and clothed.

The solution, like most solutions, came out of the blue. Why not sell Dobbin? Better still, why not have a raffle? I should make quite a bit of money that way. So, after cajoling Mam and doing a few household chores, she agreed to buy me a book of raffle tickets. The future looked rosy. For the next few nights I trudged the neighbourhood selling tickets to anyone who could afford them. One of my customers was Jack Pegleg, a huge pot-bellied man, of German origin, with a shiny black wooden leg. Jack had a reputation for having a voracious appetite, and it was said he would eat almost anything. His favourite meal was sheep's brains, including the eyeballs, and he was so strong he could flirt handles off pint pots with apparent ease.

One night after tea, with nearly every ticket sold and the takings in my secret hiding place, I separated all the counterfoils, put them in a cardboard box, and Mam drew out the winning ticket. It was Jack Pegleg's. Mam gave me an odd look and resumed knitting.

"Jack should really enjoy Dobbin," she said.

"Oh, does he like pets then, Mam?" I asked.

She laughed and nearly dropped a stitch.

"He likes anything does Jack. Especially nice tasty rabbits."

I was stunned.

"You mean . . . ?"

I couldn't believe it.

"But Dobbin's a pet, Mam, he's not for eating."

"I'm sure Jack won't bother about that, lad," she said.

With some misgivings and feeling somewhat queasy, I removed Dobbin from his hutch and carried him gently up the street to Jack's home. Immediately, as though waiting for my knock, the door was flung open to reveal Jack's huge and menacing figure. I shoved the box containing Dobbin into his grimy hands and blurted out:

"Your prize, Mr Pegleg, you've won!"

I didn't sleep very well that night. In my dreams I saw a drooling Pegleg, weilding a giant knife, whilst Dobbin, with eyes popping out of his tiny head, was running scared round and round Jack's shiny black wooden leg; and Mam in the background, laughing out loud like someone demented.

33

At school the next day I had an idea, and when the bell sounded I ran like mad. Arriving home breathless and sweating, I went straight to my bedroom. The money was gone! Panic gripped me. How? Who? I clattered back downstairs.

"Mam! Mam!" I shouted.

She was in the back yard hanging out washing.

"Whatever's the matter, lad? Why all the shouting?"

"My money, Mam, it's gone, I need it, I need it and it's gone."

"In a hurry for your bike, lad, is that it?

"No, Mam, I want Dobbin back, I want Jack Pegleg to have the money, I want Dobbin back."

She laughed.

"You're too late, Eric. Too late."

A cold shiver tingled my spine. I felt tears welling. Mam moved a snow white bed-sheet to one side.

"Dobbin's home, lad, back in his hutch waiting for you."

And sure enough, through the tears, I saw him munching away on a bright red carrot, not a care in the world.

"But how did you do it, Mam?"

"Well, after listening to you moaning and groaning in your sleep, I had a word with your Dad."

"What did he say, Mam? Is he mad at me?"

"Course not, lad. Anyway, as soon as you left for school I went round to Jack's and did a deal."

"What kind of deal?"

"The only one we could think of, lad. Your raffle money in exchange for Dobbin."

"But how did you find the money? It was in my secret hiding place."

She gave me one of her worldly smiles.

"Nothing's secret from mothers, Eric. You'll find that out one day."

The Power of Prayer

It was the coming of coal that began it all. As a community caught up in the grip of the Great Depression; life as they knew it was about to change. Not far from the cotton town of Wigan, stands a row of squalid rented houses, with the grand, perverted name of Mayflower Road. The road, cobbled and going nowhere, runs parallel to an almost defunct canal that seems to nurture bone-biting winds. It was on such a day, bleak and raw, that the coal arrived. They brought it from local pits, and dumped it along nearby sidings, where locomotives steamed and shunted industriously. Soon, a continuous black range stood stark against a grey sky. It became a talking point but no one cared: not until they found old Mrs Leeter dead. They found her wrapped in a blanket in front of a bare grate that hadn't seen wood, nor coal, for days.

Everyone had suffered the pangs of hunger, but now, with this death, warmth was almost more important than food; and the "bagger" was spawned. Whole families would form raiding parties; smash the coal into nuggets, bag it, and carry it off on bicycles, prams and homemade wheelbarrows. Then greed stepped in. This precious commodity was taken farther afield and sold for profit.

The railway company took action. They employed a security guard. This man's brutal methods soon earned him the name of "Madman" Bigalow; but the robbing went on.

In the midst of these transgressions, one family, the Fallons, stood strong: refusing, without prejudice, to yield to such temptations. With a husband and a son unemployed, Agnes Fallon took in washing, and the start of this particular week was no exception.

* * *

Topping up a bubbling boiler for the umpteenth time that morning, Agnes dried her hands and went through to the living room.

"Kathleen!"

The girl on the settee, startled by her mother's tone, sat up clutching a patchwork quilt to her throat.

"Didn't I tell you ages since to go for those aprons? I need them now; for the next wash, now get on with you."

Kathleen, pale and shivering, gripped the quilt even tighter.

"Do I have to, Mam? It's perishing out there and I'm froze stiff already."

"On your way young lady — and while you're there ask the butcher for five penn'orth of bones — and put my coat on, it's warmer than yours."

A few minutes later, father and son arrived home. With faces weathered to a ruddy glow, they stood with hands outstretched in front of the fireplace. Agnes read the familiar signs and knew instinctively that they were still jobless.

"I'll make some tea," she said. "Danny, you bring in a few pieces of coal. There's some kindling too, bring that as well."

"Where's our Kath?" Walt Fallon asked.

"I've sent her to the butcher's for his aprons — and I've asked her to fetch some bones as well."

"Hell, woman, not broth again. I wouldn't mind but there's never owt on the damn bones."

"Still, they help make a nourishing meal, that you can't deny."

"But it's meat we want . . . meat and bloody fish!"

He turned to the glimmer in the grate.

"And heat!" He said.

"If you can do any better, you'd better get cracking."

Her husband kept his back to her, shoulders hunched, staring into the fire.

Agnes poured the tea.

"I'm getting worried about our Kath, Walt; this is the second time this month I've had to keep her off school . . . she's not well at all."

"What do you expect, woman? Eh? The way we live . . . what do you expect?"

"I expect some sympathy and understanding, that's what. I can't talk to you these days without . . . without . . ."

Danny entered.

"You two arguin' again?"

As his mother went back to her washing, Danny knelt, and with the wood, roused the dying embers. Once alight, he placed the coal carefully on top.

"We'll soon be warm again," he said.

"And for how long?" His father said, staring into the gathering flames.

Danny looked at his father and could sense yet again his inner anguish. This once proud provider, now almost dependent on the fruits of his wife's labours, was suffering continually the pangs of guilt. While his father suffered, others, the baggers and their families, prospered and thrived, and it was this, their modest prosperity, that was eating away and slowly destroying him.

That night, Mrs Fallon took her daughter to see Doctor Merry. While they were out, Danny managed to rouse the fire again. On their return, flames licked and grew in strength, radiating a comforting heat. With coats away and tea brewed and poured, Agnes Fallon spoke of their visit.

"The doctor says our Kath's run-down, and that I've got to keep her off school . . . he's not happy about her chest either."

"What about her chest?" Walt Fallon said. "She's not got a cough."

"You don't need a cough to have a lung complaint . . . anyhow, he said to keep her off school, keep her warm and watch her diet."

Walter sprang to his feet, disbelief in his every utterance.

"Watch her diet . . . keep her warm . . . how the hell are we supposed to do that? The bloody man's mad!"

"Stop ranting on, you're only making things worse."

"Aye, that's it, blame me."

"Leave off, Dad," said Danny, "nobody's to blame for anything."

"Now look who's talkin' . . . you've never done much to help."

Even after all this time, his father's resentment was still obvious, still simmering, but ready to boil over into acid comment.

At seventeen, Danny Fallon was a loner who had an inborn resentment against authority and any kind of injustice. On leaving school he had been fortunate enough to find work with a local dairy. Two days later, a dispute with his foreman had led to an instant dismissal. For a family in want, the loss of a wage earner was a crushing blow; but that was Danny's way, he stood by his convictions and ignored the consequences, however devastating.

* * *

The following day, in a bid to escape the family tensions, Danny took a walk. He left Mayflower Road and headed for the canal. A few kids, oblivious to the freezing conditions, played at pirates on an ice-bound barge. It wasn't long though before the numbing cold drove him home again.

An argument was in full swing. His father's voice came through from the kitchen. Strident; adamant.

"For the last time, woman, no! There's no way that I'm facing any means test. No way!"

"But Jack Conlon went and they gave him an extra five shillings."

"Bugger Jack Conlon! I'm not going! They want to know everything about everything . . . where's the dignity in that?"

That evening, Danny and Kathleen were playing a game of dominoes. Their mother was washing up, and Walter, as usual, had sunk into one of his depressions. Suddenly, with a muttered curse, he leapt to his feet, grabbed his coat and went out, slamming the door as he went.

It was well after midnight when a loud knocking sent Danny hurrying downstairs. On opening the door, two well known baggers, Frank and John Coley staggered in supporting his father.

"Hell fire!" Danny said. "What's happened? Is he alright?"

"It's his legs," John Coley said, "he's in a bad way."

They carried him, moaning and cursing, and laid him gently on the hearth. The commotion brought Agnes Fallon hurrying in.

"Mary, Mother of Mercy! What's happened? What's happened?"

They cut away his trousers to reveal ugly bruises and lacerations to both legs.

"I think his right knee-cap's had it," Frank Coley said. "You'd better get Doctor Merry, he's in a bad way."

"I'll get my coat," Agnes Fallon said. "But how did it happen? How did he get like this?"

"This," Frank said, "is the work of Madman Bigalow . . ."

"I don't believe it. Walter would never . . ."

"Look, Mrs Fallon," John said, "your Walt came beggin' for a sack and a coal hammer, he were jokin' sayin' he were startin' his own business. After a bit, me and our Frank went after him and found him . . . just like this."

"There's not a mark on his face," Danny said.

"That's Bigalow's way," Frank said, "club and cripple — the man's a lunatic."

"But what about the police," Agnes said. "Can't they do anything?"

John laughed.

"And what do we say — stop that guard from knocking hell out of us while we help ourselves to some coal? They'll shove us in the loony-bin."

Walter's knee-cap was fractured in three places. The next morning, Doctor Merry referred him to the local hospital. Two days later Kathleen Fallon was admitted to a sanatorium. She was suffering, the doctor said, not so much from tuberculosis as from starvation. Agnes Fallon was crushed. She could come to terms with the results of her husband's foolhardiness, but her daughter was an innocent victim of poverty, and Agnes could do nothing about it.

The Fallon troubles became the high topic of conversation which brought the usual condemnations and an unwanted visitor. The night he arrived, Agnes Fallon was at the sanatorium. Father Dillon, who was both sympathetic and judgemental, sat very close to the fire.

"And how's your mother," he said. "Is she well? How is the poor woman coping?"

"She's suffering, Father," Danny said. "She doesn't deserve all this."

"Don't blame your Dad too much, Danny."

"Don't blame my Dad? What do you mean?"

"I mean, what he did . . . look what happened to him."

"He was only trying to help us."

"But he didn't help, did he? In fact, you're a sight worse off than before. I'll never understand the people of this parish."

"You mean the thieving?"

The priest nodded.

"Yes, the thieving, and the sorrow it brings."

"There's nothing to understand, Father. They steal to keep warm, and to make a few bob, that's all."

"But it's wrong, they're breaking the law, the law of God too. Do that and suffer the consequences. Look what happened to your poor Dad."

"He's not dead, Father."

"No, but his spirit could very well be."

"Unemployment broke his spirit."

"Don't let it break yours, Danny. Make your Dad proud of you."

"And how do I do that?"

"You'll know when the time comes."

"And what happens in the meantime?"

"Pray for guidance, Danny."

Danny grinned: "It might sound better coming from you, father."

"I'll do that, Danny, I'll pray for you."

Danny's grin broadened: "I hope it works, Father."

The priest smiled back: "Like many others, I think you underestimate the power of prayer, Danny."

* * *

Danny lay in bed smoking his first cigarette of the day. Five a day and his equilibrium was assured. He inhaled deeply and thought of his mother. What a life! All of her married life she had slaved at washing and ironing and cleaning, and cooking and worrying. Where had it got her? A husband lying crippled and a daughter in a sanatorium. What an existence.

After breakfast, Danny made his way to the railway sidings. A high wooden fence dotted with no-trespass signs ran the entire length of the shunting area. In defiance of these restrictions, enterprising locals, hungry for coal, had loosened planks to create a series of "doors". As Danny drew near, three of these planks swung outwards. Seconds later, a bulging bag of coal was pushed through, followed by a grunting, ferret-faced man.

"Bloody hell!" he gasped, "this is harder than workin' for a livin'."

Then with incredible strength, he threw the bag across his narrow shoulders, and ran at a jog-trot towards Mayflower Road. Danny hesitated, but the robber's bolt-hole seemed to beckon and draw him. Like a man possessed, he scrambled through into forbidden territory. Between the fence and the coal, a stretch of tall grass gave ample cover. Stooping low, he followed a well-beaten path. The coal, like some black sinuous monster, loomed before him. Some distance away to his right, he could make out a shabby, wheel-less railway carriage, and close by a fenced compound containing several jerry cans. As he drew level with the carriage. a burly man with close-cropped hair appeared. Around his neck hung a pair of binoculars. He was carrying a heavy, wooden club. So this is Madman Bigalow. Danny crouched lower. Bigalow, swinging the club nonchalantly, moved closer to Danny's hiding place.

"He knows I'm here," thought Danny. "He's been watching me."

The guard stopped a few feet away. For a man of his build and reputation, his voice was surprisingly high-pitched; almost friendly.

"C'mon, I know you're there. Out you come."

Danny stood up.

"Now you're a new one. I've never seen you before." He slapped the club against the palm of his left hand. "What're you doing here, eh? No bag, no coal hammer. What do you want?"

Danny smiled and looked past his captor. Not a soul to be seen. Just the two of them.

"You fancy your chances, don't you? I like that."

"Drop the club and I'll take you apart," Danny said.

"No way. This club is my guarantee to cripple you for life."

"I must give you credit there, you're good at that alright."

"So you've heard of me? You know something? I'm beginning to like you."

He swung the club, missing Danny's face by inches.

"Don't worry, friend, it's the legs I go for. The shins, the knee-caps. That'll stop you trespassing."

"It didn't stop him behind you."

The guard half turned. In that split second, Danny acted. A well aimed blow to Bigalow's upper arm made him drop the club. Cursing with pain and frustration he swung a left fist at Danny's head and missed.

"I don't need a bloody club," he snarled.

He lunged forward, wrapping his powerful arms around Danny's waist. His deadly embrace grew ever tighter. Danny felt his spine was about to crack. In one last desperate bid to break free, he gripped Bigalow's ears and dug deep with his fingernails. His opponent, screaming in agony, let go. Danny moved fast. Grabbing the binoculars he slipped behind his attacker and pulled hard. The strap cut into Bingalow's throat. He began to gag and clawed frantically to free the pressure. Danny thought of his father and held on grimly. Slowly, the big man's strength began to ebb. His legs finally buckled and he slipped to the ground. Danny released his stranglehold. The man who had brutalised so many lay at his feet, unconscious. Powerless.

Danny dragged the guard back to the carriage, bundled him inside and padlocked the door. A few swift strides and he was inside the compound. Grabbing a jerry can he went back up the track. As he reached the coal he began to slosh petrol. When he was finished there was a pungent glistening trail running along the foot of the range. Making a torch from the wintered grass, Danny lit his second cigarette of the day, and with the dying match ignited his torch. He walked slowly back, touching the liquid trail as he went. Soon a river of fire was taking hold. Greedy flames ate into the cobs and reached inside, into the very heart of the black mass, until there was nothing only a raging inferno.

* * *

At the corner of Mayflower Road, Danny joined the gathering crowd. Father Dillon, seeing him, pushed his way through and stood beside him. Together they watched the black smoke billow and rise into nothingness.

"Whose hand is this, Danny?"

"Did you pray for me, Father?"

"What do you mean? Of course . . . of course I did."

"Then we did it together, Father."

"I don't understand . . . what are you trying to say, Danny?"

"We did it together, Father. You, me, and the power of prayer."

The Singer not the Song

From Monday to Friday, Albert Crabtree worked down the pit. On Saturday night he put on his best suit and became a singer. A pub singer.

Lancashire bred, Albert and his wife, Brenda, lived in the middle of a row of rented houses, not far from Wigan Pier. Albert was a natural. He'd never had a singing lesson in his life, but by 'eck, his tenor voice was a joy to hear. It was even suggested that he was good enough for the Wigan Hippodrome. Such was the quality of his singing.

Every Saturday night, before leaving home, Albert would go through what had now become a ritual. His tea was a light meal of eggs, bacon and black pudding; then, with a smart nod to Brenda, he would pay a visit to their outside toilet . . . "just to clear his pipes" — and the sound was beautiful. The lavvy chains shook and rattled and the water gurgled as he gave his neighbours an impromptu rendering of his favourite song "Danny Boy" — and nobody sang it better.

When Albert, from the confines of his closet, cleared his pipes in preparation for a coming concert, his powerful and melodious voice could be heard streets away, rising and falling, rising and falling, with wonderful clarity.

People would travel miles to be thrilled by his magnificent tones. Charabas would be turned away, as fans, having heard of his next venue, packed the building to bursting point. And Albert loved every minute. The adulation was like an aphrodisiac. He attracted females, young and old, like flies to a kipper. And it was no wonder. His vibrant voice and his singer's poise made him a target for their amorous advances. And, as a typical example of the male of our species — weak and unreliable — Albert became a willing victim.

Brenda Crabtree loved her husband, body and soul. There was no one else to love. Her parents were dead and she was an only child. She didn't work but saw to it that Albert lacked for nothing in comfort or requirements. She knows her husband's weaknesses and made allowances.

On Saturday nights while Albert was doing a concert she would slip next door and keep Mrs Woodcock company; sipping tea and listening to the radio. And of course, gossiping. But she never failed to be back for Albert. With his supper in the oven and his slippers on the hearth, she suffered in silence and prayed fervently he would come straight home. On certain Sunday mornings, when she found lipstick on his collar, she worried even more, but said nothing. She loved him and could never imagine life without him. Besides, there was no alternative. She was a one man woman, married for life.

* * *

The envelope on Brenda Crabtree's doormat was brown in colour and without a stamp. Brenda's name was printed on the front in pencil. The letter inside, also in pencil, was short and to the point.

MRS CRABTREE KEEP YOUR EYE ON YOUR HUSBAND. I SAW HIM LAST SATURDAY AFTER HE'D DONE HIS CONCERT. HE WAS SAT WITH A RED-HEADED GIN SWILLING HUSSY. HE'S A GREAT SINGER IS BERT AND HIS DANNY BOY IS OUT OF THIS WORLD. BUT BELIEVE ME THAT RED HEAD WAS MORE INTERESTED IN THE SINGER NOT THE SONG.

At the bottom of the letter, in even bolder print, was the word BEWARE.

All day long Brenda's mind was in turmoil. What should she do? How many more letters would come through the door? Should she burn the letter and forget all about it? After all, having a drink with a woman didn't mean he was having an affair. All day long her thoughts ran riot; until, at last, she reached a decision. That same night, just as Albert was finishing his tea, Brenda took away his plate and placed the brown envelope in front of him.

"What's this?" Albert said.

"Read it and see," Brenda said.

"But it's yours," he said.

"We've no secrets, have we Albert? Read it."

Albert took out the letter and read it. Without the least show of emotion, with not a flicker of an eyelid, he said:

"What does it mean, love?"

"It's plain enough to me, Albert. Actually, it's quite straight forward."

"But surely you don't believe this . . . this rubbish."

"Oh, and why not?"

"Because it's some spiteful old bitch trying it on. It just isn't true."

"Oh yes it is, Albert, oh yes it is."

"All right, all right, I was doing a bit of flirting, but I know her . . . it's all innocent stuff. You know, just for laughs."

"I'm not laughing, Albert."

"It won't happen again, love, I promise."

"I know it won't Albert, I'll make sure it doesn't."

"How do you mean, love?"

"I'll be with you at every concert, Albert. Everywhere you go, I go."

"But you don't drink, love, and you've nobody to go with. You'll be bored."

"I'll be singing, Albert."

"Eh? What do you mean, Love, singing?"

"Singing . . . with you. We'll be a singing duet."

"Hellfire!" Albert said. "You can't sing, Brenda, you'll destroy me."

"Have you ever heard me, Albert?"

"Funny enough I haven't . . . but . . . "

"Mrs Woodcock, next door, thinks I'm quite good."

"Uh, Mrs Woodcock's eighty-three and deaf as a doornail, how would she know?"

"My mind's made up, Albert. I'll leave you to do the organising. But don't drag your feet, I'm getting quite used to the idea. By the way, how does The Singing Crabtrees strike you?"

"Hellfire!" Albert said.

Albert, expecting Brenda to forgive and forget, did nothing. On the last day in March, Brenda cooked her husband his usual meal then disappeared upstairs. A few minutes later, his meal finished, Albert made his way to the back door. Even in these times of stress, Albert never failed to clear his pipes.

"How do I look, Albert?"

Brenda was standing at the bottom of the stairs. The dress she wore, glittered and sparkled like a Christmas tree. Albert swallowed hard.

"Going out, Love?"

"Tonight's the night, Albert. Just think of it — The Singing Crabtrees — we'll send them wild."

Like a zombie just risen, Albert went down the yard, entered the lavatory and closed the door. Once again that rich and powerful voice echoed with a haunting beauty from yard to yard, from house to house. Never before had Albert's voice reached such a crescendo. Neighbours stood spellbound, waiting, waiting, for that final top note. But it never came. That final effort to clear his pipes had proved too much. Albert had sung his last song.

At Albert's funeral the priest ended his eulogy with these words:

"Albert Crabtree was a wonderful man with a wonderful voice that was surely a gift from God. The voice and the man belonged, not to any one person, but to each and every one of us."

And Brenda Crabtree sobbed and sobbed and felt guilty for the rest of her days.

Born to Fight

It all began in France on the 13th of April 1918. A stray machine-gun bullet found its mark, just missed his windpipe, and left him close to death. Six weeks later he was shipped back home to Blighty to recuperate. With his strength and mind restored a return to the trenches was an almost certainty. But it wasn't to be. Before he was fully recovered the war came to an end.

He married and started a family, and to those outside the family circle, all seemed well; unknown to them however, the trauma of that near-death experience had done something to him. A deep-down anxiety tormented him. A feeling of vulnerability made him suffer. Aches and pains became incurable diseases. Problems, domestic and otherwise, magnified and became — to him at least — insurmountable. His doctor, who could spot an hypochondriac three miles away, gave him friendly advice, told him not to worry and ushered him out.

Then came the years of want. He took his turn in the ever increasing dole queue and worried even more. Disillusioned and desperate he sought solace in books and became an avid reader of Zane Grey's wild west novels. Gradually, as if in defiance of his common upbringing, he became . . . well, more studious. His books were now of the medicinal kind. Herbal books of every description cluttered his home. He would spend hours and hours making notes and studying finely drawn illustrations and photographs. One day someone gave him a Nicholas Culpepper edition. Large and leather-bound it was packed with every herbal cure known to man. And it changed his life completely.

With time of no importance, he would set out from home, follow the Leeds to Liverpool canal and onwards to adjacent woods and meadows. These havens of nature became the gathering grounds for whichever herb took his fancy. With every passing day his knowledge increased and his general well-being flourished. The fresh air and long walks in the countryside became the cure for all his unfounded ailments.

Spurred on by these bodily and cerebral improvements, he went a step further. Using precious household money he made three purchases. Number one, a chest expander, number two, a punch-ball, complete with two pairs of boxing gloves, and last, but to him, as equally as important, one pair of Indian clubs; not your lightweight, juggling kind, oh, no. These were solid, polished mahogany ones, weighing four pounds each, and guaranteed to make your shoulder muscles stand out like coconuts.

Shortly aher this physical and mental transformation, this self-taught herbalist, this reformed hypochondriac, this man — my Dad — took another giant step; he became Frank Danby's trainer. How this came to be I shall now reveal, because I was there every step of the way. And when I look back I wonder about the miracle of things. About the actions and events that spring from nothingness and help to shape and mould a person's character. His very soul even.

* * *

I first met Frank Danby in the summer of 1936. It was the first week of my school holidays. Dad had brought him to our humble abode for the first of many a simple teatime meal. His introduction was short and to the point and in a tone of — take him or leave him, it's up to you.

"This is Frank Danby, folks, he's a mate o' mine and he does a bit o' boxin', don't you Frank?"

"Sort of." Frank said.

He certainly had the look of a boxer. His face was still unmarked, but his shoulders were wide and seemed out of place above the rest of his body. His stomach and hips were practically non-existent, giving the impression of speed and agility. His navy blue suit was shabby and ill-fitting, but did nothing to hide his power and simmering vitality.

"Who do you box for?" Mam said.

"He trains at Barney the Turks place, don't you, Frank?"

"You mean that ramshackle dump across the common?" Mam said.

"That's it. Barney's gym. He's a good man is Barney." Dad said.

"Do you make plenty money?" Mam said.

"He doesn't get paid." Dad said. "He just trains there and fights when Barney says so . . . But his time'll come, won't it Frank?"

"Where do you work?" Mam said.

"He doesn't." Dad said. "He's like me, he's on't dole."

"And he doesn't talk much either, does he?"

Mam's dry, off the cuff remark had the three of us in stitches and brought her third degree questioning to a halt. After tea Dad gave Frank a tap on the shoulder, followed with a knowing wink.

"C'mon upstairs, Frank, I've got somethin' to show you."

"Can I come too, Dad?" I asked.

"Just as long as you don't make a nuisance of yourself."

Mam and Dad slept in the back room which Dad had turned into a makeshift gymnasium. His Indian clubs stood in the far corner near the window. The leather punch-ball was suspended between ceiling and floor and behind the door hung his chest expander. A chart on the wall gave the following information. A CHEST EXPANDER COURSE by ALFRED DANKS FOR THE ATTAINMENT OF HEALTH, STRENGTH AND DEVELOPMENT. And below this heading were fifteen black and white photographs of a very muscular Danks in various stages of exercise with carefully worded instructions of starting positions, movements, and finishing positions.

"By 'eck," Frank said, "you've got a gym of your own here, mate . . . By 'eck."

"Aye," Dad said, "I like to keep in shape."

And then he proceeded to demonstrate his ability in the art of club swinging. After a few minutes of vigorous exercise he passed the clubs to Frank.

"Here, mate, you have a go."

But Frank was hopeless. In an effort to emulate dad's dexterity he gave his right knee a bang that made him grunt with pain, crashed the clubs in mid-air and clipped his ear, and finally, after nearly knocking himself unconscious, he gave it up.

"Show him how it's done, Eric." Dad said.

Using one club only, I swung it in front of my body, up and over and behind my shoulder and down again in a sweeping motion in front of me. Then I brought the second club into play. Twirling one after the other in rhythmic movement, I could see that Frank was impressed and swung them ever faster.

"C'mon, Eric, stop showin' off. That's enough." Dad said.

After a few more attempts, Frank managed to get the hang of it. Before he left that night he made a vow to be the best club swinger ever born.

* * *

One Sunday forenoon, Dad, keen to divulge his knowledge of herbs and plantlore to us lesser mortals, took Frank and me on one of his country excursions. We left the canal bank near the village of Rookam and followed a narrow grassy track by the side of a small copse and onwards to hedge-bound verdant fields and meadows, where tall, purple foxglove and cow-parsley pushed and shoved their way ever upwards towards a blue cloudless sky. Before long, Dad had the both of us mesmerised with the names, cures and healing qualities of every plant in sight. Two hours later, hot, tired and hungry, we left behind the smells and sounds of this rural seclusion and made our way back.

Halfway across Gambler's Field we met the elder brother of the Kelso family, Vic Kelso. Vic was short in stature, but broad and fleshy looking, with a bald head and a cauliflower ear. His piggy eyes took in the three of us then came to rest on Frank. His scrutiny of dad's friend was both slow and calculating.

"You're lookin' fit, Frank. Getting many fights?"

"Not by a long chalk," Frank said. "I could do with more, that's for sure."

"You'll wait for ever at Barneys, he's got them queuing up, you know that."

"His turn'll come," Dad said.

"Not wi' Barney, it won't," Vic said. "An' dole money's not much help, is it Frank?"

"You don't think much o' Barney, do you Vic?" Dad said.

"No I don't, he's killin' the fight game round here. His methods are slow and he's always full o' promises. Tell me, do you know of one fighter . . . just one, mind, who's done good at Barneys. Eh? Eh?"

The animosity between Vic Kelso and Barney the Turk was a regular topic of local gossip, which never diminished or lost any volatility in the telling of. Barney — a man of dubious nationality, hence his title — was an ex-army physical training instructor, and a staunch advocate of the Marquess of Queensbury rules, who had formed his own club on leaving the forces.

Vic Kelso was his complete opposite. His headquarters was the back room of the Three Crowns pub and consisted of three members only. Vic and his two younger brothers, Norman and Wilf. And all three fought like tigers. They took on all comers, any race, size or religion. And the rewards were instant. Various opposing pubs who also promoted their own fighters, came to mutual, monetary arrangements, and sometimes a purse of two hundred pounds exchanged hands. Hand-picked referees and seconds usually received their rewards in the form of foaming tankards and cigarettes. Occasionally, the more brutal form of bare-fist contests was agreed upon as this never failed to attract even more spectators.

"How would you like to earn a few quid, Frank?" Vic said, with a thin smile.

"Doin' what?"

"Doin' what some folk think tha good at. Boxin' . . . Fightin'."

Frank shrugged his broad shoulders and looked at Dad and the look said. Help me out, mate. Say something. Advise me.

"Tell you what," Vic said. "Fight me I'll make it a one way purse. Fifty quid if you put me away. What do you say?"

"And what's in it for you?" Dad said.

"The satisfaction of flattenin' one of Barney's so called, up and comin' champions. That'll do me."

"It's a deal." Frank said.

"Now just a minute . . ." Dad said.

"There's one thing," Vic said. "Leave the gloves at home. Let's give the crowd value for money. A match they won't forget; eh, Frank?"

"Now just a minute," Dad said again, but nobody was listening.

* * *

The word spread like a forest fire, and the following Sunday morning on Gambler's Field saw a large gathering of locals and non-locals buzzing and speculating and laying bets as to the outcome of the coming event. The one person missing was Barney the Turk. On hearing that one of his star pupils had taken up the Kelso challenge, Barney had promptly barred Frank from using the club's facilities and crossed his name from the register. Dad took over where Barney had left off, and all that week leading up to the confrontation, Dad's instruments of torture; chest expander, clubs and punch-ball were used extensively. And just to pile on the pain, Dad borrowed a battered bicycle and acting as pacemaker had Frank pounding the canal towpath every dawn for five consecutive days. The day prior to the fight Frank was allowed to rest and spent the time ingesting some of mam's nourishing menus.

The day chosen was fine and warm. Frank changed his clothes at our house and Mam found an old dressing-gown for the short walk to the field of battle. I was responsible for transporting water, clean towels and a bucket. We arrived to a somewhat rousing, derisive cheer. Police lookouts had been posted. There was no ring. A seething square of blood-thirsting humanity made up for the lack of ropes. Two wooden beer crates acted as stools. The Kelso clan had already arrived. Vic was on his feet, jumping up and down and punching fresh air. He was shorter than Frank and his body, now gleaming with sweat, though fleshy, was well-formed. His bald pate and hairless physique made him look invincible and very dangerous. In comparison, Frank looked like a college graduate. Thick black hair crowned dark handsome features. A sculptured body and a boyish demeanour that looked almost gentlemanly inside this ragged arena of pending combat. A tall red-nosed man, who looked as though he was suffering from an hangover, had been chosen to referee. He now glanced at both fighters in turn and beckoned them to the centre of the ring. Dad gave Frank an encouraging back-slap

"Go get him, Frank!"

The referee, without any introduction, spoke to both contestants in low, inaudible tones. Then, with a sharp nod at the two seconds, he lifted his voice above the bedlam.

"Right! Let the fight commence."

To the roar of the crowd both men began a slow cautionary circle, throwing tentative, weak jabs. Urged by the spectators they became more probing and vicious. Frank, crouching low, went in fast, broke through Kelso's guard, and pummelled his stomach and ribs. Vic gasped with pain and back-pedalled from the ferocity of his opponent's attack. Frank, over confident, dropped his hands. Kelso retaliated going for his unguarded face with a speed that belied his bulk. One blow sent our man reeling back into the crowd. He was held upright and pushed back to his adversary. The two men came together. They stood, toe-to-toe swapping lefts and rights to body and face.

"Give it to him, Vic!" shouted a Kelso supporter. Dad and me too were shouting wild and unnecessary instructions.

"C'mon, Frank, you've got him beat!"

"Go for his face! Watch his left!"

The crowd was going wild, baying like hounds after the spill of blood. After what seemed like an eternity, the round ended. Dad and me worked fast. Frank's right eye was swollen and his nose was bleeding badly. We gave him water, doused him and wafted cool air on his bruised body.

Round two. The two fighters met and battled on with ferocious intensity. More bruises. More blood. Round three. Frank made another torrid charge at Vic's midsection and followed up with a tremendous right uppercut that nearly took his head off. Kelso was sent sprawling and lay like a dead man on the trampled grass.

While the referee was counting the slowest one to ten that I'd ever heard, Norman Kelso dashed into the ring and threw water on his prostrate brother. Before reaching the count of ten, the two seconds brought the round to an end. Dad and me protested loudly but were shouted down by everyone but Frank himself. Round four. Vic, now fully recovered, went in like a wild man. Frank didn't stand a chance. Vic's weight and hammer-like blows pummelling an already abused and battered torso were just too much. Frank was poleaxed. His body could take no more punishment. He couldn't get up. While the crowd went berserk and lifted the victor shoulder high, Dad and me managed to get Frank to his corner. His face was a terrible mess. His eyes were closed. His nose split and gory and his body from neck to waist a fiery red with cruel knuckle marks.

When we finally got him home, Mam sent for doctor Merry. The good doctor could do very little. There were no broken bones. Iodine and salve for his many lacerations were prescribed. But Dad had other ideas. That same afternoon Dad took me on one of his herbal excursions.

"We'll soon have Frank back in fettle again," he said.

"What are we looking for, Dad?"

"Knitbone."

"Knitbone? That's a funny name."

"Knitbone, nipbone, bruisewort and boneset, they're all country names which have been given to a herb with the proper name of comfrey."

"And what will it do?"

"It'll have young Frank lookin' like a new man again."

And sure enough Dad was right. The comfrey was brought to the boil, simmered for twenty minutes and the juice used to bath Frank's injuries. For the more serious ones Dad made poultices from the wet leaves. A week of continuous applications and nature's healing properties had worked wonders. Frank's many battle-scars had all but disappeared.

But it wasn't over. Frank's right eye was giving him trouble. A visit to the eye hospital was arranged and the results were devastating. The message was loud and clear. Competitive boxing had to stop immediately or suffer the consequences. Frank entered into a period of depression. We wouldn't see him for weeks and in that time I would miss him like a brother. The dole queue grew and the fight game for him was over. There seemed no solution to his dilemma.

* * *

One Saturday morning, Dad and me were sparring in our backyard. Frank came down the entry and stood watching, hands in pockets, slouched against the wall. Dad, out of puff, saw his friend and grabbed his chance to take a breather.

"C'mon, Frank, show this young bugger how it's done."

"Those days are over, mate, you know that . . . you know what the hospital said."

"Hell, Frank, our Eric's not tall enough to do any damage . . . besides, it's only a friendly lesson tha givin'."

Reluctantly, Frank pulled on the gloves and Dad laced them. Three rounds later Frank's enthusiasm was blatantly obvious. His eyes shone. His face glowed. His instructions decisive and encouraging. That Saturday was the beginning of Frank's revival. And Dad didn't miss any of the signs

"That'll do for now," he shouted. "How about another go tomorrow, Frank, eh?"

"I might come down," Frank said. "Just depends."

In the meantime Dad took me to one side and gave me a few terse instructions. The next day, Frank, who couldn't resist Dad's invitation, had the shock of his life.

Half the kids of Mayflower Road were waiting patiently for their first free boxing lesson.

From that day on Frank Danby never looked back. Every weekend, undernourished, but eager lads queued to box with a man with a mission. A man who had been beaten by dubious methods, who against all odds, had made an alternative comeback, and his fame spread. So much in fact, that Barney the Turk on hearing of Frank's setback and recovery and his dedication to the teaching of local kids, hired him to teach those same kids, free of charge, at his own gymnasium and paid him a sufficient wage for doing so.

Dad had lost his protege, but he too had required a reputation. Frank forever grateful to his friend became a go-between. Anyone sustaining injuries that didn't require medical attention, were promptly referred to the care and attention of Dad and his herbal remedies. Even the Kelso brothers came knocking and Dad's only payment was friendship and gratitude. And these two most important assets made him a happy, contented man.

* * *

Although his courage was never in doubt, the lure of money had almost destroyed Frank Danby, but his willingness to push aside his own problems and to help his own kind to mature into proud, strong and disciplined men of tomorrow had given him an incentive. A fresh start in life. And that was the Frank Danby I knew and admired. A born fighter.

Brotherly Love

Like me, the Copple brothers were born and raised in Mayflower Road, and their school was my school; a rough Catholic school, where the headmaster, Hector Wainwright, ruled with fist and cane, where blood ran freely and the pupils, afraid of both right and wrong, lived in fear of his violence.

Frank Copple was older than his brother Tom. Strong, swarthy and pugnacious, the pair feared nothing and no one except, of course, Owd Hector Wainwright.

Their strength, looks and combined wildness, even for two brothers, was almost uncanny; but there the similarities ended. Frank, the eldest, lacked his brother's intelligence, imagination and coordination and was considered by all who knew him as — slow on the uptake. Frank was something of a misfit, whose poor grasp of words and numbers was a constant parental worry. Even so, most parents in these times of poverty thought that a job, however menial, was far more important than any intellectual qualifications.

It is not to be assumed by all this that Tom was a clever clogs, far from it; but what he lacked upstairs, Tom made up by being physical. He excelled in sport. His specialities being, rugby and swimming. Therefore

Owd Hector for ever aware of any talent that would enhance the schools' and his reputation, made certain that Tom was given all the support necessary. With the rugby season over and another trophy in his display cabinet, Hector was looking with great expectations towards a second piece of silverware, a magnificent shield inscribed with all the names of the victorious schools.

In just a few weeks time a clash between the favourites, St Benedicts and his own school would see his ambitions realised. Tom was on top form, and Owd Hector, confident that his star swimmer would leave the rest floundering, slept easy. Such was his confidence, Hector, who when certain of a win, liked to have the odd flutter, bet Mr Lonsdale, the head teacher of St Benedicts, £5 pounds, on the outcome.

But before all this came about, the elder Copple, thankful to escape the miseries of maths and English, left school, and we, Tom and me, moved into Owd Hector's class.

* * *

One Friday noon, Owd Hector was busy chalking up some mind-boggling sums when through the door staggered Frank Copple carrying a batch of brand new exercise books. A murmur of recognition ran round the room.

"It's Copple, he's got a job."

"It's Frank Copple, the lucky sod's found work."

"How did he get a cushy number like that?"

"By 'eck! he's still wearin' short pants."

The din drew the attention of Hector, who, on spinning round to vent his wrath recognised the instigator.

Frank, somewhat pleased by all this attention, gave a broad smile, plonked the books on Hector's desk and turned to exit.

"Well, well, well," Hector's tone dripped acidic. "If it isn't Frank Copple. My, my. Got a job, then, have we, Frank?"

"Yes, sir, I'm workin' for Maxwells, sir."

"Ah, yes, Maxwells. So, you're a delivery boy, eh? Good money?"

"Er, no, sir."

Hector moved closer to his trembling victim, and as he did so his nose began to twitch.

"Hmm, is that tobacco I can smell, Copple?"

Frank cleared his throat. "No, sir."

"Are you calling me a liar, Copple?"

"No, sir, I never did, sir."

"Show me your hands, boy!"

Now ashen faced, Frank's remaining confidence plunged to his grubby socks. He took a step back and put his hands behind him.

"Show me your hands, boy!"

Hector's voice, loud and menacing, rattled around the walls. Everyone held his breath. I glanced across the aisle. Tom Copple's face, like his brother's, was a sickly white; but there was also an unmistakeable presence of hate about him. I could almost smell it. I watched and waited. He was gripping a ruler with such intensity his knuckles too, stood proud and as white as his face.

Surely he would step in. He couldn't just sit there and watch his slow-witted brother be humiliated. But he did.

Slowly, nervously, Frank brought his hands to the front of his body, and held them, fingers outstretched, for all to see. Dark and nicotine-stained, his digits trembled and shook.

"Empty your pockets, boy." Hector rasped.

Frank did so, brought forth several packets of foreign cigarettes, and placed them on Wainwright's desk.

"Good God!" Hector said. "This is 1942, boy, there's a war on, where did you get all these?"

Frank shrugged. "Up and down, sir."

"How many times have I warned my class about the dirty habit of smoking, hmm? Yet still you do it."

"But I've left school, sir."

"But you ve been a pupil of this school, Copple, and I expect you and everyone else to set an example, to show the rest what a good school this is, and what have you done? You've let us all down, Copple."

"Yes, sir."

"You know the punishment for letting me down, don't you, Copple?" He reached for his well-used cane, "Bend over, boy."

There followed gasps of disbelief and the shuffle of bodies as the whole class strained to see the final humiliation of Tom's brother.

Surely this would break Tom's resolve. Surely he would intervene. But he sat like a statue, pale and immobile, staring intently at the ruler which he still held in a vice-like grip.

The ordeal over, Frank Copple, fighting back the tears of humiliation, walked slowly, painfully, to the door, and out into the spring sunshine.

* * *

The big day arrived. Spectators — including the mayor and mayoress — came from far and near.

Apart from Owd Hector's side-bet — which was now common knowledge — a local, church-going businessman had promised Wainwright's rugby team a brand new strip if St Benedicts were soundly beaten, and, as a personal boost to his generous donation he was now seated next to Hector, red-faced and talkative, puffing away on a fat cigar.

The tannoy boomed. The swimmers filed out and took their positions by the pool; rolling heads, shaking limbs, loosening muscles and nerves. With just one exception. Tom Copple stood still and flaccid. Impervious to the echoing shouts of encouragements, standing as though waiting for a number 9 bus, he stared straight ahead. Then, with a sudden shock of realisation I knew that Tom Copple was determined to lose. And I knew why. This would be the ultimate sacrifice, a sacrifice tinged with the sweetness of revenge.

Owd Hector would lose everything. His bet, the promised rugby strip, and more than all this, his dignity.

Reluctant to witness this sacrificial act of retaliation, I left the building.

* * *

Knowing Hector's reputation, I feared the aftermath of Tom's actions. But my fears were groundless. With just weeks to go before school leaving age, Tom played truant, leaving Owd Hector ranting and fuming and cursing forever, a brave act of self denial, all because of brotherly love.

The Liverpool Invaders

When Herr Hitler began his blitzkrieg on England's major cities, Winston Churchill and his cabinet devised a dramatic plan of evasive action; a mass exodus. Kids from every shell-blasted, burning town in the kingdom, adequately armed with suitcase and gas mask were whisked away to safer climes. They left Liverpool, London, Belfast and Portsmouth. They invaded north, south, east and west, and places abroad. Our invaders came from Liverpool.

* * *

The bridge that spans Mayflower Road is just a whistle away from one of Wigan's busy stations, which means, inevitably, a busy signal. A red signal means a stationary train which also means a trail of carriages stretching way back to our humble bridge. And in those waiting compartments sit the bored victims of our begging calls from the road below.

"Chuck a penny out!" . . . "Chuck a penny out!" . . . "Chuck a penny out!"

Windows are lowered, heads appear, coins are thrown, and we below push and scramble and bicker like young savages as brass and silver rain down, bouncing and rolling before us like jewels in the sun. A threepenny bit hits my shoe and careers off over slippery cobbles, straight into the greedy, grimy hands of Marion Connor.

"You lousy bitch, Connor, that's mine . . . Give it 'ere, you thievin' swine."

"Find yer own . . . I found it first!" She snarled, and pounced like a cat on another rolling penny.

Anger raised more aggression. I push and elbow my way to the front and look up, scanning faces and windows in the hope of catching some sympathetic eye. Two tousled heads appear. Two impish grins. A momentary pause. A flash of hand. I squint into the glare of the midday sun. The shock of impact takes my breath. A big juicy tomato lands smack in the middle of my face: hanging there like a second nose before slipping away down to the front of my brand new jersey. I felt bilious with pent up anger and shame and strike out blindly at sneering, laughing faces. Scraping pulp from my face I glare upwards just in time to see a wide grin topped by a thatch of red hair duck quickly back inside the carriage. The train's whistle blew a warning and began its slow progression. The two heads reappear. The owner of the red one touched the tip of his nose with a forefinger and gave me a Churchillian vee sign.

"It's a good job you're on that soddin' train," I thought.

The excitement over and still penniless I hurry home. They were burying Mr Holly at one-o-clock and Mam wanted me there, showing what all dead people should be shown: respect.

As with all funerals, the neighbours of the deceased had turned up in force. I managed to find room near a corner gas-lamp. The hearse and one attendant car were already in position, waiting sombrely for that dreadful hour. I was just about to shin up the lamp for a better view when mam's voice filtered through the congregational chatter.

"Eric . . . Eric . . . come 'ere, quick!"

The next thing I knew she had me by the hand, urging and pulling me along.

"C'mon, lad, we're goin' to have a last look at Mr Holly before they box 'im."

Those very words conjured up all kinds of mental images. Alarm bells told me to break lose and flee, but knowing Mam's temper, common sense prevailed.

At the door of the Holly's house, solemn, black-suited men filed past us carrying wreathes and bouquets to the waiting hearse.

With shaking legs and an even shakier heart, I allowed Mam to lead me forward into the dark interior. The coffin, suspended on two trestles, lay under a heavily curtained window. At its head sat a red-eyed Mrs Holly. An empty cup and saucer rattled gently on her lap. Mam took the crockery from her and tapped her gently on the shoulder.

"Our Eric's come to pay his last respects, Mrs Holly," she whispered.

But I hadn't. She'd dragged me there. I didn't want to see Mr Holly. I'd never seen a dead person before and I didn't fancy seeing one now. Not now, not ever. Mrs

Holly looked at me with red moist eyes and nodded, trance-like.

"Go on lad, before they come for him."

Mam gave me a hard nudge: "Go on then, pay your last respects, 'urry up."

I moved hesitantly over to the pine box. What would he look like? Was I supposed to say something? Say a prayer? Kneel, or what?

With great trepidation I peered into the coffin, looked quickly away and back again. I stared harder and was almost certain I could see his lips move. I went giddy and weak. This body sapping weakness seemed to magnify the sounds around me. The sobs of an old woman. The laments of a man. I was overcome with the injustice of it all. Everyone, but Mr Holly was alive. Speaking, crying, hearing and laughing. A surge of grief rose from deep within me, and came to my lips, but not as sorrow or tears. For some unknown reason I began to snigger. I couldn't help myself. In this, my state of weakness, I had succumbed to one of the most sacrilegious acts of human nature ever known, I was laughing in the presence of death.

I covered my face and dug my nails deep into the flesh of my cheeks. The pain steadied me. I heard the voice of Mrs Holly.

"Poor soul — he's heartbroken — what a nice lad."

I felt Mam's hand on my shoulder and keeping my head low followed her outside, out into the life-giving heat of a midday sun.

A little while later the coffin and cortege moved sedately along Mayflower Road, under the bridge and out of sight. Cloth caps were replaced, tears mopped and normality resumed. Conversation returned to everyday topics. Familiar characters shuffled, spat, smoked and spoke of this and that. Mr Holly was forgotten.

As the crowd began its slow dispersal I heard this strange sounding accent, loud, odd and provoking.

"Hey, our kid," the voice said, "there's old tomato face."

And the laughs that followed made me wince and squirm with embarrassment. It was the duo from the train. They each carried a case and gas mask; brown identity tags dangled from their coat lapels. Between them stood our parish priest, Father Dillon, a protective hand resting on each unruly head.

"These two young men," he said, addressing Mam, "are the Cary brothers, Samuel," he patted a red head gently, "and his little brother, Paul. They're from Liverpool — the bombs, you know . . . They've been taken in by the Holly family."

"Bad timing, I must say," Mam said.

"Yes indeed," the priest said thoughtfully. "I wonder, could you possibly take care of them? . . . That is, until Mrs Holly returns."

Mam, fully aware of the barrage of glares and challenging stares that had been fired from both sides became tactfully diplomatic.

"Tell you what, Father," she said, "I'll take them round there, Mrs Croston's there now making sandwiches and things, we can find them something to do."

"Excellent idea, don't let them demolish all the food though, goodness me, no."

Without further ado, Mam led the two Liverpoolers away but not before me and the red head had given another two way display of intense dislike.

* * *

For the youthful males of our neighbourhood, Mayflower Road and its unpleasant surroundings is a fabulous but dangerous playground. Almost daily there is some new adventure, some daring challenge that is an integral part of having to live within the confines of a socially depleted area. And within these dangerous but exciting confines several warring gangs fought for supremacy. Each of these groups had a name; usually the surname of its leader. But mine was called the Ericson gang. It had a certain ring to it, which to me anyway, seemed to signify the desperados of the old American west.

Obviously, any leader worth his salt, always led by example. Never, in moments of danger, or any other trial of character should his leadership ever be questioned. I know, because, Jimmy "Jimbo" Hornby, Billy "Birdy" Briggs and Terry "Colly" Collingwood, always expected — and duly received — the very best in leadership qualities. I had learned the hard way, using tact, diplomacy and a fair amount of grit and determination. In the face of danger I had excelled, and the others had recognised it as courage. A courage which I had always taken for granted, and never for one moment did I ever dream it would desert me; but it did, and in the most appalling circumstances that I had ever known.

* * *

Mrs Holly had just two addictions, Kendal Brown snuff and Wild Woodbine cigarettes and Jimbo and me did both errands, Jimbo for the snuff; me for the cigs. For Mrs Holly, Fridays were special because it was our job to deliver enough snuff and fags to last the weekend. On this particular Friday my delivery was late and it was teatime before I finally tapped on Mrs Holly's front door and entered. The three of them, Mrs Holly and the Cary brothers were sat down to a meal of Lancashire hot pot.

"I've brought your cigs, Mrs Holly," I said.

"You're a good lad, Eric, just leave them on the table."

And after a rummage in her battered old purse, produced a shiny new penny as a reward. The brothers, intent on devouring the contents of their plates, ignored me completely.

Giving my thanks but glad to be leaving the swelter of her living room, I made a hasty exit. It was a well known fact Mrs Holly suffered from "thin blood" and always "kept a good fire".

I'd only gone a few yards when the brothers caught up with me. Sammy gave me a poke in the back and in that funny accent said:

"Somebody sez you've got a gang."

"Who's tol' you that?"

"Never mind who, me and our kid want to join."

"You'll be lucky."

"What's so good about your gang, eh? . . . Tomato face."

"Nowt to do wi' thee."

"Think yer big, don't cher?"

"Big enough."

"You've never had a German bomb dropped near yer."

"What about it?"

"You'd 'ave shit yoursel'."

His ginger head came within a menacing inch of my face.

"It'll tek more than a Gerry bomb to get on my gang," I bragged.

"Such as?"

"Never mind."

His brother, Paul, gave a tug on Sammy's sleeve and whispered something. Sammy nodded in agreement.

"Ever seen a piece of shrapnel?" he said.

At the outbreak of war I had begun to collect army badges and now owned a grand total of six. I'd never seen a piece of shrapnel and that very fact made me feel inferior. I had a sudden urge to see and feel a piece of a real German bomb.

"No, I've not," I said reluctantly. "Why?"

"I've got a lump," he said triumphantly.

"I don't believe thi."

"You can 'ave it if me and our kid join thi gang."

My thoughts ran riot. Just imagine. I'd be the only one in Mayflower Road. The very thought sent my heart helter-skelterring out of control. I thought hard.

"Tell you what," I said. "If you give me the shrapnel and pass some tests, I'll let you in."

"That'll do us, won't it Paul? When do we start?"

"Give me the shrapnel first."

"Oh, no, you get that when these so called tests are finished."

"They won't be easy," I said.

"Make them as hard as you like," he said defiantly. "And don't worry you'll still get your bit o' bomb."

That very same night I called the gang together to plan the most devious and dangerous of tests we could think of.

A couple of days later, Jimbo, Birdy, Colly and myself called on Mrs Holly. The Cary brothers were playing a game of Ludo.

"Well, ready for your first test?" I said.

"What's it to be?" Sammy asked.

"You'll see, just follow us."

* * *

Paxton Lock had a weir. To reach the weir was easy; cross the lock bridge, step onto a dividing tract of land and the only obstacle between you and the opposite bank was the fast running weir. Now there's only one way to cross that water — apart from swimming — and that is by walking across an half-submerged length of timber just four inches wide. We had all talked about doing it, but the actual deed never seemed to present itself. We were now about to witness a first attempt.

On our arrival the weir was uncommonly high, running fast and all but covering the slippery timber. I gave the brothers their instructions and allowed just one concession; they could if they wished walk the plank barefoot, but they must do it fully clothed.

"Is that it?" Sammy said.

"That's it," I said. "Just two crossings, there and back."

"C'mon, Paul," Sammy said. "I'll go first."

Sammy sat on the bank, slid down the side onto the slimy wood and with his bare feet fore and aft, began to walk. Balancing like a high-wire artiste his precarious traverse was slow, and I must admit, heart stopping. If Sammy overbalanced, the weir, which was on his left, was strewn with old prams, bicycles and discarded bedsteads, all waiting to maim or spear his unresisting body. Not once did he take his eyes from the wooden beam. On reaching the other side he leant against Walton's perimeter fence to rest a while, then made a slow agonising return. And believe it or not we all gave him our sincere congratulations. I was so relieved; I decided, as gang leader, that enough had been done and gave Paul permission to abandon the challenge.

Sammy, now bristling with confidence became somewhat cocky. "Was that the hardest you could think of, Tomato Face?"

"That was an easy one, bloodnut, wait till you come to do the next."

"When's that then?"

"Tomorrow. Meet us on Gambler's Field at ten-o-clock . . . and don't be late."

"I'll be there," Sammy said, with a grin.

* * *

Because of their produce, Calman's bone works was teeming with rats. Countless families survived on a diet of bone-meal and animal fats, and left the confines of Calman's for one thing only; water. And close by the works lay their oasis; Bulrush Pool. Early morning and late at night, dozens of the vermin drank their fill at the water's edge and then scurried back to a labyrinth of tunnels to eat, sleep and breed relentlessly.

Late in the day of Sammy Cary's balancing act I led the gang down to Calman's factory, located a few rat-holes, laid wire snares and went home to bed.

A return visit on the following morning revealed the full extent of our catch. Three had been garrotted, but a fourth had been snared by an hind leg, which was just the result I was hoping for. We were lucky really, because a rat will normally chew off a trapped limb to release itself — this one obviously had had second thoughts. Wearing a pair of leather gloves I freed the squealing victim, tied a piece of strong cord to its tail and shoved it inside a cardboard box.

With punctilious timing, Sammy and his brother met us at the arranged rendezvous.

"What you got there, then?" asked Sammy truculently.

"Inside this box," I said, "is your second test."

"What is it," he sneered, "a pair o' clogs wi' nails stickin' through?"

I placed the box on the grass and removed the lid. The rat, somewhat confused, came wandering out, the string trailing behind. I watched the colour drain from his face and knew this was the clincher. He would never pass this one.

"Ugh! Its a bloody rat! Kill it!"

"Take your shirt off." I ordered. "Why, what're goin' to do, eh?"

"Take your shirt off and lie down."

"No way. Not wi' that bloody thing about."

Birdy Briggs, who was holding the rat in check, broke out into a manic laugh.

"What's the matter, tough guy? Scared of a little rat, eh? Some tough guy."

"What're goin' to do?" Sammy said again.

"Take thi shirt off an' see," I said.

"I'll do it." Paul said, stepping forward. Then without any further prompting, began to strip.

Stunned and grieved, I said, "Are tha sure?"

"Don't be daft, Paul," Sammy shouted. "C'mon let's get away, they're bloody mad, the lot o' them."

But Paul, keen to show his boldness, said "Well, what do I do next?"

"Just lie down and keep very still," I said.

Paul did as I bid and lay down in the cool, rich grass.

"What now?"

"I'm goin' to let the rat run over thi body."

He made no reply, but I saw him clench his fists till the knuckles went white.

"Right," he said grimly. "Get on wi' it."

Dangling the rat over Paul's bare chest I lowered it gently onto his belly. He began to laugh.

"What's he laughin' at?" Colly asked.

"He's shit scared, that's why," Jimbo replied.

"It's feet are ticklin' mi," Paul laughed.

I eased the tension on the string and let the rat crawl up to Paul's chest.

"That'll stop thi laughin'," I said.

"Take it off! Take it off!" His brother shouted.

"It'll kill 'im! It'll kill 'im!"

"Shud up!" Paul shouted back. "Shud up!"

But by now Sammy was almost hysterical. Grabbing the string from my grasp, he snatched the rodent from his brother's body, twirled it round his head a few times, and let go. The rat flew through the air and landed close by the canal. Birdy ran over, picked it up by the tail and threw it in the water, leaving it to swim for the opposite side.

Revenge, they say is sweet and for me it was exceptionally so. I'd scared Sammy half to death and that to me was the sweetest thing ever, but I must admit he rode the taunts like a trooper. The condemnations just bounced off him.

"I don't like rats," he said simply, and that was that.

But his couldn't care less attitude only made me more determined to make him suffer further indignities.

Another meeting was called. Once again our feelings were mutual. Because of Paul's untimely intervention we all agreed unanimously that his big brother should be given an even tougher assignment, and each had the task of thinking up the worse possible situation.

But our would-be machinations proved fruitless. A terrible twist of fate capulted my hated adversary to the dizzy heights of heroism, which left me very shamefaced and repentant.

* * *

Because of her "thin blood" Mrs Holly always kept a good fire. Summer and winter alike she stoked, poked and cared not one jot. And because of her indifference, the Cary brothers, whose only means of escape meant frequent street games and visits to the cinema, decided on a very warm day in 1941 to accompany me and the rest to an afternoon at the pictures, leaving Mrs Holly to an afternoon of self indulgence. In the quietude of the afternoon, Mrs Holly fell asleep, when — or so it was assumed — a piece of burning coal fell to her rug. The flames took hold. The widow slept on.

When we arrived home a crowd had gathered to watch, advise, speculate and query.

"Somebody get the fire brigade, quick!"

"I wonder how it started?"

"Where's Mrs Holly?"

"Bloody hell! She's still in there."

Suddenly, Sammy, who was standing next to me, was pushing his way to the front, elbowing and knocking people to one side.

"Where're you goin'?" I shouted.

But I knew without asking. If Mrs Holly was still inside that burning building, Sammy was going after her. I knew this and froze on the spot. I wanted to go with him, but I couldn't. My legs became leaden. They wouldn't move. In other words, I was frightened to death.

With a swift kick at Mrs Holly's front door, Sammy, bending low, plunged into the smoky interior.

"Bloody hell!" Someone shouted. "That lad'll get killed."

"What's he playin' at?" Another yelled. "Silly sod!"

Amid the din of popping glass and burning materials, I could just make out the sound of an approaching fire engine. Just at that moment a yell went up.

"He's got her! The young bugger's got Mrs Holly."

Bent double under her weight, Sammy staggered to the pavement. Many hands went to his aid. Mrs Holly was laid gently on the flags. As Sammy retched and coughed over her prostrate form, the fire fighters arrived. Hoses appeared. Uniformed personnel dashed hither and thither, all intent on doing their duty. One went over to Sammy and Mrs Holly. He knelt awhile, giving close attention to the victim. After a few minutes he stood up, said something to Sammy, shook his head and beckoned for a blanket. The body of our neighbour was gently covered and moved away.

The days that followed left every one in a kind of unbelievable stupor. In just a whisper of time a childless couple had vanished for ever. A gutted house and memories the only proof that they had ever existed. Consolation for the Cary brothers came in the shape of Father Dillon. Acting on behalf of some higher authority, he placed the two lads in the care of a devout catholic spinster who resided close to his church. And that was the last we saw of them. And I for one was very relieved. You know, being the leader of a gang is a very precarious business, especially when you've been upstaged by a ginger-headed, freckled-face scouser who showed us all what bravery really is.

But that wasn't all. Just to aggravate matters, I never did get to own that piece of Gerry shrapnel. It was thrown out with the rest of Mrs Holly's incinerated belongings.

Two of a Kind

They schooled and grew as friends but were destined by time and events to become bitter enemies.

Malcolm Fenton was the clever one. He won a scholarship, went to grammar school, joined the police force, moved house, married and produced a son. Samuel Neill, left school with not a credit to his name, signed on the dole, stayed in Mayflower Road and stayed single.

Once in uniform, Malcolm, fastidious and dedicated, became obsessed with promotion. His colleagues, knowing of his aspirations, gave him a wide berth, for it was Malcolm's intention to use anyone as a rung to climb his ambitious ladder.

Samuel, his complete opposite, lived in a different world. His only aim in life was to be the master of his own fate. To achieve this, he became self-employed. Using local tips as gathering grounds he salvaged discarded bicycle parts and with time of no importance, transformed his collection into gleaming, glossy roadsters.

A small deposit and the lucky buyer became a proud owner of a genuine, Samuel "knocker" Neill special. With a system of reasonable weekly payments from his clientele, Knocker was always guaranteed his daily bread and of course his packet of woodbines.

But money, even in small quantities, was hard to come by and many a dole man wanting the luxury of a Knocker Neill Special resorted to lawless ways of paying their dues.

Not far from Mayflower Road and stacked high above the curve and gleam of numerous shunting lines, lay the very source of their unlawful income. Great cobs of coal all freshly mined from local pits.

Ferried to and fro by wagon and loco, the supply and demand for this essential fuel was never ending and it was there for the taking, but with the taking came risks. Avoiding the clutches of the ever vigilant railway detective was one of them. Another, more menacing obstacle was the bobby on the beat, whose name happened to be, Sergeant Fenton. With many a capture to his credit, Fenton's reputation became established. And for the thieves there followed chaos and profitless days. Something had to be done, so when Mayflower Road's most infamous crook made a clandestine delivery to the home of Knocker Neill, he took the problem with him.

* * *

Grateful for a restocked coal-bunker, Knocker offered freshly brewed tea and toasted crumpets, which was an invitation Charlie Tinwin couldn't refuse. With margarine running down his ample chin, Charlie gave voice to his worries,

"I don't know when you'll see the next lot, mate."

"How come?" Knocker asked.

"Well it's bad enough dodgin' them railway blokes, but that pal o' yours, he's a right un, he is."

"Pal o' mine? . . . Oh, you mean Malcolm Fenton. He's no pal o' mine, Charlie."

"That's 'im, Sergeant Fenton, that's the bugger!"

"The sod'll make Chief Constable one day, I'll bet," Knocker said.

"He's a sod all right. He seems to know every move we make."

"That bad is it?"

"Aye. Turn a corner an he's theer, nip through an entry an' he's bloody waitin'. It's uncanny."

"That's because he knows every street, every nook and cranny. Local knowledge, that's what it's called, Charlie."

There was a short silence as Knocker's visitor bit into his third crumpet and slurped more tea.

"Aye, he knows every street an' every flamin' entry."

More silence. More slurps as Charlie took advantage of Knocker's hospitality.

"There is a way round it," said Knocker thoughtfully.

"Oh, an' what way's that? Ask 'im to come an' join us?"

"Lookouts."

"Lookouts?"

"That's what I said, lookouts."

"I don't follow thi."

"Okay, Malcolm Fenton knows the area, but so do you . . . If not better."

"I still don't follow."

"It's simple," Knocker said. "If you carry on from the bottom o' Mayflower Road where do you end up?"

"Past bone works an' straight into the canal if you don't watch what you're doin', everybody knows that."

"Right. Put a lookout near Calman's bone works an' he can see right over to Elston Bridge. Agree?"

"That's for sure."

"Now then, coming from town how many streets lead direct to Mayflower Road?"

"Hang on, I'll 'ave to think about that."

"There's two," Knocker said. "Afghan Street and Preston Street. Am I right?"

"I think so."

"So that tells us you only need three lookouts. One at Calman's, one at the top of Afghan Street and one near the railway bridge on Preston Street. It's as simple as that."

"But he's got a bike."

"Then beat him at his own game. Three lookouts, three bikes . . . you can't lose."

"I don't know." Charlie said. "That will mean three of us not gettin' a fair share o' coal — it wants some thinkin' about."

"I'll be a lookout," Knocker said.

"You?"

"Why not? Just keep me supplied wi' free coal, that'll do me."

"You're not kiddin', are you?"

"Which means you've one less to bother about, get the rest to take turns and your problem's solved."

"You mean like a rota system?"

"That's it, where nobody loses out."

"By thump, you're talkin' about are organised gang, aren't tha?"

"Why not? It's the only way you'll get the better o' Fenton — By the way, a lookout at the shuntin' lines might be a good idea, too."

"Good thinkin', mate; but we'll 'ave to keep mum . . . you know why, don't you?"

"Oh, I think so," Knocker said, with a smile.

"I don't think tha does. Did tha know Fenton's lad knocks around wi' our Billy?"

"No I didn't."

"Well, he does, so we'll 'ave to tread careful."

"We'd be daft not to," said Knocker grimly.

"Do you know summat?" Charlie said. "I never thought in a million years it would come to this."

"To what?"

"You an' Fenton on't opposite sides, you used to be two of a kind, you two."

"That was many moons ago, Charlie, many moons."

* * *

The summer days were long and hot, but in no way did they discourage the demand for coal. Preparing for the coming winter was a never ending process and the storage of cheap fuel was undertaken by everyone. And with the demand, the "scramblers" as the gang came to be known, found fame, notoriety and a regular source of income. Knocker's plan of surveillance had assured that, and he being the only non-scrambler, had the pick of lookout points and his choice was always Calman's bone works. Positioned on Gambler's Field at the rear of the factory his watch on Elston Bridge was an easy task.

Only once did he spy the uniformed sergeant wheeling his sit-up-and-beg across the canal. With powering legs and pounding heart he raced madly to warn the scramblers, who, having various means of escape, vanished from the scene taking their ill-gotten gains with them.

With an obvious fall in captures and convictions, Fenton became suspicious and decided to call on the railway company. A few days later stringent tactics proved to be a success and several arrests were made. Among them was a relative of Charlie Tinwin.

The scramblers went into hiding and Fenton armed to the teeth with crucial evidence, went to see his one-time friend. Knocker, unaware of a pending confrontation answered the door.

"Afternoon, Sam, how've you been?"

Knocker, quick to regain his composure, looked up and down the street and held out his hands.

"Quick! slip the cuffs on before somebody comes."

Malcolm smiled weakly: "Still the same . . . Still the joker."

"Somebody's got to do it," Knocker said.

"Can I come in a minute?"

"As long as tha wipes thi feet."

Malcolm removed his helmet and followed Knocker inside.

"Sit thi down, sergeant."

"There's no need to be formal, Sammy."

"That theer uniform makes things formal."

"I think you know why I'm here, don't you, Sam?"

"If it's a recruit tha after, I'm not interested."

"I know all about your little caper, Sammy."

"You mean mi little business? — well it's all legal and above board, ask anybody."

"We've got Sy Masters in custody, he's informed on you, Sammy."

"Simon Masters? What's owd Sy got to do wi' me, sarge?"

"You're in serious trouble, Sammy."

"What're you goin' on about?"

"Aiding and abetting, that's what I'm on about."

"Aidin' and what?"

"I'll throw the book at you, Sammy."

"Make sure it's a dictionary I were never any good at spellin'."

"Next time I'll have a warrant?"

"What kind o' warrant?"

"To search your workshop."

"You'll find nowt theer only bits o' owd bikes and such, hang on I'll get the key, you don't need any bits o' paper."

"No need for that."

"Please thisel."

Sergeant Fenton stood up, his neat, uniformed figure looking curiously out of place amongst the clutter of Knocker's living quarters. And when he spoke his voice was softer, almost fatherly.

"Isn't it funny how time changes things?"

"You mean us? Thee a bobby an' me what I am?"

"You've strayed, Sammy, you used to be all right."

"There's nowt wrong wi' me sergeant, it's thee what's ended up all high and mighty."

"I'm still the same, Sammy, I know my roots."

"That's were tha wrong, Mr Policeman. That uniform 'as made thee a class apart. Tha knows thi roots, but tha lookin' down on us all."

"I've never looked down on my kind, never!"

"T'other day," Knocker said. "Somebody said we were two of a kind, me and thee, Uh! We might o' bin once."

"I've got a job to do, Sammy, and a family to support."

"So tha 'as. I wonder if that lad o' thine'll change?"

"Now there's were you're definitely wrong. Infact he comes down this way to play."

"So I believe, but if he comes to thy way o' thinkin' owt could 'appen."

"He knows good from bad and right from wrong, I've made quite sure of that."

"I'm sure tha 'as," Knocker said. "Anyway, sorry I didn't offer thee a cuppa, but I only serve it to friends."

* * *

Every Saturday Richard Fenton was given permission to visit the local cinema and every Saturday, without fail, there would be at least one film featuring cowboys and Indians. After which, all the kids of Mayflower Road, including Richard, re-enacted the parts played from start to finish. And what better place than Gambler's Field. For on that field of play, cropping the lush green grass, was reality itself. His name was Jimmy and he was a piebald pony belonging to Jed Coop, the neighbourhood rag-and-bone man. With their young minds still fresh with the heroic deeds of their screen idols, each one took turns to ride the reluctant animal. When boredom set in the dares began. When it came to young Fenton's turn, the tethering rope used as something to grip, was now abandoned. Climbing aboard the pony's back, Richard drew two imaginary six-shooters and urged the beast to gallop, but Jimmy, tired of giving free rides to these unruly, make-belief cowboys, refused to budge. Billy Tinwin, impatient for a turn, gave the reluctant horse a smart slap on his rump, whereas Jimmy, not wanting another of the same, shot off at great speed. The suddenness of it all took the policeman's son by surprise and he crashed with a sickening thud on the ground. The laughter soon turned to commiserations as the gravity of Richard's fall was realised. Surrounded by a sea of worried faces, the victim, milk-white with pain and shock, pleaded for help. Billy Tinwin, keen to make amends, raced off in the direction of Mayflower Road. The rapid arrival of Doctor Merry was soon followed by the noisy commotion of a speeding ambulance. The broken flesh and protruding bones had told the good doctor everything. Young Richard had suffered compound fractures to both legs.

Two days after the accident, Knocker Neill had another visit from Charlie Tinwin. Over Woodbines and strong tea they exchanged news and views.

"I see owd Sy's back in circulation," Charlie said.

"Uh! That doesn't surprise me," Knocker said.

"You can't really blame 'im." Charlie said. "Owt's better than jail."

"Is it?"

"You'll be okay. Fenton's got nowt that'll stick, he's only Sy's word for it."

"He's still comin' wi' a warrant."

"What for? What will he find? Sod all. You've done no thievin', everybody knows that."

"Like tha sez, I've nowt to hide," Knocker said. "It's just the humbug of it all."

"He's enough problems of his own without pesterin' thee."

"Oh?"

"Didn't tha hear abaht 'is lad?"

"His lad? What about him?"

"Broke both 'is flamin' legs ridin' Jed Coop's pony. I thought everybody knew."

"First I've heard."

"It's true. Had breaks too I believe. They reckon he's stuck at home and won't come out."

"What's stoppin' 'im . . . he can use a wheelchair, somebody'll push 'im."

"Won't use one, sez he's not a baby, they reckon he's gettin' proper depressed, poor little sod."

When his caller had gone Knocker made a second brew and stared unseeingly at his daily newspaper. With the tea consumed he rummaged around found some notepaper and a pencil and spent some time making sketches and notes. With each drawing his mood improved, until, with a final flourish and a satisfactory smile, his scribblings came to an end. The results of this artistic activity was now followed by long hours spent in his shed and from which there came the muffled sounds of industrious goings-on. Finally, one week later, silence reigned and Richard Fenton's friend, Billy Tinwin was sent for and ushered inside Knocker's workshop. Neighbours stood in silent bafflement as from within they brought wooden panels, rubber tyred wheels, rods, nuts and bolts and a steering wheel. After two hours of diligent work, the assemblers stood back to admire the fruits of their labour.

"What is it?" Someone asked.

"A wooden car." Someone answered.

"It's a sledge." Another said.

"A sledge doesn't 'ave wheels, you daft sod."

"But it's got a platform at the back just like one."

"It's still not a sledge. It's got two mirrors and a steerin' wheel."

"And there's room inside to carry things," Knocker bragged.

"Who's it for?"

"It's for mi mate," Billy Tinwin said. "And I'll be shovin' 'im round init."

"Everybody'll want that job," someone said. "Just imagine goin' up a steep hill an' jumpin' on that platform . . . Great!"

And so it was. Young Fenton overwhelmed and overjoyed with Knocker's unique creation, became his old self. With his postilion friend at the rear, they traversed the neighbourhood in happy abandonment that only kids of an irresponsible disposition can fully appreciate.

* * *

Time moved on and the prosecution of Knocker Neill never materialised. Rumours ran rife. The Chief Constable, through lack of evidence, had shown mercy.

Certain members of the force had been receiving stolen coal. But the most popular theory was Knocker's humanitarian act involving a certain sergeant's son. Whatever the reason the scramblers of Mayflower Road heaved a sigh of relief and carried on as usual. Once again the conflict of wit and guile between the jobless and the authorities gathered momentum.

Knocker Neill, however, opted for a better way of life and gave his full attention to the designing and improving his latest invention with the hope that one day his idea would bring him recognition and monetary gain.

But he still received his free coal. Billy Tinwin and Richard Fenton saw to that. It was the sergeant's son who first got the idea. With Billy at the rear he would steer his way to the sidings, where, under the pretence of watching the industrious wagons and trains, Billy, armed with a sturdy knapsack would gather just enough nuggets to be secreted by the side of Richie's plaster cast legs.

All went well until the suspicions of a keen railway official led to their downfall. Lying in wait he chose the opportune moment, pounced and made his arrest.

"I've seen some odd things in my time," he said, "but never anything like this."

He produced a notebook: "What's your names? Where do you live?"

Billy gave Richie a sly wink: "My name's Billy, my Dad's a vicar."

"Oh, aye. And I suppose he's your brother."

"My name's Richie," Richard said, "and my Dad's a policeman."

"Aye, and I'm the mayor of Wigan."

"It's true," Billy said, "his Dad's a police sergeant: honest."

The guard, newly appointed and still unsure of himself, hesitated, then made a snap decision. Putting away his notebook he pushed out his pigeon chest and said:

"Right! copper's son, vicar's son, it makes no difference to me, you're still thieves; still two of a kind and acting as an authorised detective of this railway company, you're nicked!"

The Suit

Money, someone once said, is the root of all evil. It's an irrefutable fact, men have killed for it; and died for it. It is the most elusive of possessions man has ever known. Ask a poor man, he'll tell you.

Where I lived back in the thirties, everybody was poor. And it showed. Living standards were reflected in a variety of ways. Rented hovels with one cold water tap. Outside blocks of dilapidated closets and a dull, unvarying diet that was the norm for one and all.

But the biggest giveaway of this dire existence was blatantly obvious. Armies of clones trudged our cobbled streets. Men in dark, creased jackets, baggy trousers and cloth-caps. Women wearing clogs, shawls and pinnies; and kids dressed in long-sleeve jerseys, short pants and knee-length grey stockings. Everyone looked drab and colourless. To ease domestic pressures nothing was thrown away. Children's clothing was passed down through the family brood. Clogs refitted with irons, shoes soled, jerseys and socks darned; knitters knitted and on cold winters nights hessian sacking was pegged and patterned into colourful hearth rugs.

So that's how it was with us poor folk. Make do and mend, pass it on, hand it down. There was no end to it.

To eke out an already miserly pittance some people went into debt and the pawnbroker prospered.

Our Norman was far too young for hand-me-downs and me being the one and only "big brother" had never had any. Not until Mam received that brown paper parcel all done up in sealing wax and string with a maple leaf motif stuck to it.

* * *

In the top drawer of our highly polished dresser, there was kept a fat black leather wallet. Inside of which there was pictorial evidence of family, friends and relations. Some of these relations were extra special. They were Canadians. Every photograph — black and white, of course — showed my far away cousins, parents and all, frolicking around in snowbound landscapes, tobogganing down slippery slopes and throwing ubiquitous balls of snow. I was insanely jealous. They looked so happily carefree, rich and well-dressed in chunky, stylish coats, mufflers and mittens. God I was jealous. At night I would go to bed, close my eyes and will myself to dream of Canada and my Canadian cousins. But I never managed it. The nearest I came to that distant land was by gazing wistfully at those black and white photographs. But all that was about to change.

Mam was a great writer of letters and her frequent correspondence to Nova Scotia were always long and gossipy, with equally long and numerous replies, often followed by some small gift of woollen mittens, socks and the odd scarf and I must admit, all very welcome to a family who had nowt. Then one October Friday in 1937, that brown paper parcel arrived.

"Here you are, Eric," Mam said. "Wash your hands and try this on."

I paused in the act of mopping up the last of my cod and chip tea. Draped over her bare arm was what looked like a brown suit.

"What is it?"

"A suit. It's come all the way from Canada. It's a good un too. Come on, wash your hands and try it on."

"What do I need to wash mi hands for?"

"Because they're full o' grease, that's why."

"Do I 'ave to, Mam? I was goin' out to meet mi mates."

"Not before you've tried this on you're not."

It was no use arguing so I sprang into action. At this particular time of the year collecting wood for our coming bonfire was about the most important thing in the world. But I was going nowhere. The suit wouldn't fit. I struggled and grunted like mad as I tried to squeeze into it. The trousers were so tight I feared castration. The jacket too, rendered me incapable of any free movement. Mam's gaze was one of unconcealed admiration.

"Ooh, it's lovely . . . I bet it cost a lot of money."

There was no doubt about it, the material looked and felt expensive. The jacket had patch-pockets, a small belt at the back, with short, high lapels and had five buttons. The long trousers, complete with leather belt, had no turn-ups and sported, not one, but two hip-pockets. The brown, small check pattern, caught in the glow of our evening fire, had a sheen that comes, not with wear, but from quality. Not in a million years could we ever afford such an outfit.

"Ooh, it's lovely," Mam said again.

"I'm not wearin' it," I said.

"What! . . . What do you mean, you're not wearing it?"

"Like I said, I'm not wearin' it."

I began to sweat pounds and moved away from the fire. I tugged at the jacket.

"It's too tight, Mam, it's killin' mi."

"Don't be daft, it fits like a glove."

I fumbled with the belt and blew hard.

"Soddin' hell, Mam, it's two sizes too little."

"There's nowt wrong with it. Leave the jacket unbuttoned. And if you swear again I'll clout you one."

"And what about these, eh? I tried my best to lean forward. "Look, these pants are a mile too short. I look gormless."

She knelt in front of me and gave both pants legs a good downward pull.

"I might be able to lengthen them a bit."

"And what about here?"

I forced my legs apart and indicated the region of my genitalia.

"I won't be able to pee."

"Cheeky monkey . . . many a lad would go crazy for a suit like this."

"I'll go crazy if I don't get it off and quick."

"I want you to keep it on till your Dad gets back."

"Oh, Mam!"

"Sit down, he won't be long."

"I don't think I can, Mam, and if I do I won't be able to get up."

"Now stop exaggerating and sit down."

Just then in walked Dad carrying our Norman. On seeing me standing to attention, red-faced and sweating buckets, he nearly dropped my brother on his head.

"Flamin' 'eck, what's up with 'im?"

"What do you think, love?"

"I think he needs a doctor," Dad said.

"What do you think about the suit . . . the suit?"

"Tell her Dad . . . tell her it's too little."

Dad laughed: "It's either that or you're too big, lad."

"Stop jokin' Dad, and tell her."

Dad gave our Norman to Mam and took a closer look.

"Put it this way," Dad said. "If he breaks wind he'll take off like a flamin' sky-rocket."

"Right! That's it. Off it comes and I'm wearin' it no more."

Unperturbed, Mam said: "It'll be all right with a few alterations, you'll see."

And I did see. Even after Mam's deft needlework the second try-on was just as bad. The pants were still inches too short and clung to my lower regions like a second skin. Moving the coat buttons hadn't helped much either. But Mam was still adamant.

"It's a crying shame if it's not worn," she said firmly.

Mam decided there and then that I would only wear it on special occasions. Sunday mornings, visiting relatives and on festive holidays. When that first Sunday came round I complained of a sore throat and whispered my wish to stay in bed. Surrounded by comics and supplied with numerous bowls of bread and hot milk laced with butter, I enjoyed one of the best Sunday mornings of my life.

On the following Friday I went to confession. In the gloom of the cubicle I could just make out the profile of Father Dillon, our most ardent priest. With only a prison-like grille between us I felt very vulnerable and exposed. Although his gaze was averted I was sure he was aware of my identity. I tried to disguise my voice.

"I have a confession to make, Father," I said in a gruff voice. Silence.

"Last Sunday I told my mother a lie and missed coming to mass, Father." Silence.

"I said I was ill, Father, but I had a good reason."

"Go on, boy," the priest said.

"You see, Father, it's like this."

And I poured out the whole story, emphasising, of course, my deep down fear of ridicule. My tale told and feeling better for it, I waited for Father Dillon's response. The silence was unnerving. I wondered if he had nodded off. I now felt like an idiot. Why had I come? Whatever priestly decision was made I was sure Mam would overrule him. Mam was the lawgiver in our house. At last, his voice, low and almost melodious, filtered through the grille.

"And you say your mother's alterations made no difference whatsoever?"

"None, Father."

"Hmm, you do realise to be disobedient is to sin. The Fifth Commandment states categorically: Honour thy father and thy mother: that thy days may be long upon the land which the Lord thy God oweth thee . . .

which simply means obey your parents every wish . . . however . . . "

I waited with baited breath for his decision.

"Have you approached your father about this?"

"He seems to think it's all a big joke, Father."

"I think you should have a quiet word with him. Sometimes fathers can be most perceptive and very understanding."

"Yes, Father . . . I'll do that, Father . . . Thank you."

"For your penance you will say five Hail Mary's and five Our Father's before going to sleep every night for a week."

"Yes, Father . . . Thank you, Father."

"And see a doctor about that throat."

Then with great deliberation he gave his blessing and drew the small green curtain to imply that my confession and his words of wisdom had come to an end.

* * *

Saturday's weather was still consistently fine and after dinner, Dad being a fresh air and exercise fanatic, set off to stretch his legs. It was a great opportunity for Father Dillon's suggested tete-a-tete, so I kept him company. We crossed Elston Bridge and stayed on the canal towpath. Breathing deep the country smells I made my move.

"I went to confession yesterday, Dad."

"Oh, what have you been doing wrong then? Nowt bad I hope."

"I told Mam a lie about bein' ill t'other Sunday, so I went to confess."

"I don't think God'll strike you down for that, lad."

"I told a lie because I didn't want to wear that suit, Dad."

"I don't blame you son."

"You don't?"

"I must admit, I think your mam's goin' a bit too far this time."

"Then why don't you tell her?"

"Because we've got to bide our time, lad. That clobber's come all the way from her sister's lot in Canada, if you don't wear it she'll feel as though she's let them down . . . Do you understand?"

"And what about me, eh? I'll be the laughing stock of Mayflower Road."

"I know, I know — Leave to me, I'll think o' summat."

"That's what Father Dillon said."

Dad stopped dead in tracks, gave me a quizzical look and scratched his head.

"I've just realised summat."

"What's that. Dad?"

"Just what a crafty little beggar I've got for a son."

There was no answer to that.

* * *

With still a few days to go before bonfire night, it was a busy time. Every year, we, the Mayflower Road gang, took pride in building the biggest and best fire in the whole area and it was an honour we always strived to maintain. Every night after school — weekends included

— the collection of all things flammable took priority. There was nothing more important. Not until Mam dropped another bombshell.

"We're going visiting this Sunday, Eric, and I want you in that suit . . . I'll have no excuses, all right?"

The threat of that simple statement once again sent me into a well of depression. In desperation I looked across at Dad immersed in his evening paper. What had happened to his promise? Leave it to me he had said. Uh! Some Dad. I hated him.

Saturday arrived. After our midday meal Mam took young Norman round to grandma's. I went collecting bonfire stuff, leaving Dad engrossed in one of his favourite pastimes, reading a western novel.

There was no sign of Dad at teatime, and Mam, complaining about his lateness, put his food in the oven. Half an hour later Dad made an entrance carrying a large, gilt-framed picture; a panoramic view of some idyllic rural setting.

"What have you got there?" Mam said.

"A present for you, love."

"What for? What have I done to deserve this? . . . And how much did it cost? . . . And where did the money come from?"

"Which do you want me to answer first, love?"

"The last one, where did you get the money?"

"How do you know it wasn't given to me?"

"Because nobody in their right mind would give away something like that . . . Where did you get the money?"

"I've put something in hock, love."

An eerie silence followed. I held my breath, waiting
for the coming wrath. Our family never, ever went to a
pawnbroker. What we didn't have we managed without.
This was an unspoken family rule, and to break that rule,
well . . . Mam's voice came down a menacing notch or
two.

"And what, may I ask, have you put in pawn?"

"Eric's suit."

Even in this intense moment I felt a thrill of anticipation
run through my body. I couldn't believe my ears.

"And where did the picture come from?"

Mam's measured tones momentarily took the edge off
my surging euphoria.

"Well, I was paid five quid for the suit and I gave
Jemmy Pickup four pounds and ten shillings for the
picture. I thought you'd like it, you always wanted
somethin' for that far wall."

"You mean you thought you'd soften me up . . . I
know what's goin' on, I'm not daft. Where's the ten
bob?"

Dad placed the note on the table.

"There you are, love."

"And the broker's ticket, where's that?"

"In mi top pocket."

"Right!" Her voice rose again. "Take that there picture
back to wotsit, get your money back and go and collect
Eric's suit . . . now . . . this minute."

"It's too late" Dad said. "They're shut."

Mam turned a plum red with anger and frustration.

"Hand over that pawn ticket . . . come on . . . this
minute."

Dad, somewhat shamefaced, put the offending piece of paper on the table beside the ten shillings. Mam folded them together and tucked them in her purse.

"Now take that — that painting back to . . . Jemmy Pickup and get your money back."

"He won't like it," Dad said.

"If he makes it to the Three Crowns with our money, you won't like, and that's a promise."

Dad realising the errors of his ways made a quick exit.

Later that night, with the painting back with its rightful owner and money and ticket secure in Mam's purse, the volatile atmosphere returned to normal. At least Dad had managed to get me a reprieve. With the suit in hock Mam's plan for showing me off to her sister and family was now in tatters. Later still, while Mam was making supper, I managed a furtive whisper.

"Thanks, Dad."

He winked: "I tried mi best, lad, I tried mi best."

First thing Monday morning my determined mother hurried round to the pawn shop and retrieved my two-piece. The owner, amazed at the rapidity of the transaction agreed not to charge any interest.

Once again my pride was in dire jeopardy of taking a depressing plunge. And it wasn't long in coming. On the last Sabbath day before bonfire night, Mam's wish to see me dressed up in that brown, Canadian suit was finally fulfilled. With a blush on her cheek, and what looked like a tear in her eye, she saw me off to church.

* * *

That Sunday morning I suffered a form of penance that even Father Dillon on a bad day would never have bestowed. Even now, many years later, I can see and hear those glances, smirks and sniggers from passers-by and from a supposedly friendly and God fearing congregation. I chose a pew at the rear of the church and was glad I did so. I performed every physical movement in slow motion as I struggled to kneel and rise and pass the collection box. Even making a sign of the cross was an effort. Afraid of splitting my pants at the alter rail, I decided against Holy Communion.

After the service I made my way home through the backstreets and alleyways. I couldn't wait to remove this hateful, offending second skin. But even the best of intentions don't always materialise. The greeting was short and to the point.

"You can leave that on," Mam said, "your dad's taking you and our Norm to visit Auntie Bea, it's warm enough and the walk'll do you good."

The only consolation I could glean from this parental command was the fact that Aunt Beatrice lived only three miles away and the shortest route was along the canal and over the River Douglas and through the countryside.

As we crossed the Leeds to Liverpool a boatee of an horse-drawn boat gave us a friendly wave. A few minutes later we left the towpath and tramped through long grass to a second bridge. Wigan's River Douglas, like the canal, was once used to ferry coal, stone, flax and cotton; but eventually fell victim to modernisation and with its demise came deterioration, turning one of

111

our town's once navigable waterways to just an open sewer.

The closer we got, the stronger the stench that rose and wafted on a warm gentle breeze. Halfway across the aged wooden bridge, our Norman, overcome with a sudden fit of adventurism, broke away from dad's grip, made an unsteady dash for the other side, tripped, fell and rolled like a human ball under the bottom rail and into the shallow, weedy water below. Dad, without a moments hesitation, climbed between the rails, hung momentarily from the structure and dropped close to his struggling infant. Panic stricken, I ran from the bridge, down the river bank to the water's edge. Dad, holding our Norman above the foul smelling ooze, was making a slow, undulating headway through water and slime towards me.

"Throw me summat, lad. Quick!"

I grabbed the branch of a nearby bush and tugged and twisted for all I was worth; but it was hopeless.

"Hurry up, lad!" Dad shouted. "Try something else."

There was nothing else for it. Off came the jacket. Keeping a firm hold of one sleeve, I waded out as far as I dare and flung the coat towards them. Dad, stretching out his free hand managed to grab the other sleeve.

"Well done, Eric! Now pull like hell! Go on, pull!"

Sinking, slipping and sliding, I did my best, but my strength was ebbing fast. Just then, two weekend walkers, fully aware of our predicament, rushed to our aid. Smelling strongly of drink and cursing all the while, our two slightly tipsy saviours soon had the three of us, gasping, muddy and smelly; but highly grateful, onto dry land.

Our ordeal over and both men duly thanked, we made our way home. Stinking like broken sewer pipes and somewhat bedraggled, we drew some lingering, inquisitive stares from many a Sunday stroller.

On arriving home Dad led us down the entry and into the communal yard. A lift of the latch and a shout for help soon had Mam hurrying to the backdoor. After the initial shock of seeing her whole family slime covered and smelling foul, she went into action. Leaving Dad and me on the doorstep she carried our Norman indoors and inside twenty minutes had him washed and dressed and shining like alabaster.

One hour later with the three of us spick and span and smelling strongly of carbolic soap, Dad gave Mam the full story.

After recovering from the typical reactions of a concerned wife and mother, she said, with a worried frown:

"I'm going to have quite a job on getting Eric's suit clean, I must say."

Dad, seizing the moment, rose to the challenge.

"And what about mine and Norman's, love, what're you goin' to do with them?"

"Oh, they'll have to be thrown away."

"And what makes our Eric's any different? Besides, it'll fall apart before you get rid of that pong, I'll bet."

"I suppose you're right," Mam said. "But it's a crying shame . . . a good suit like that . . . a crying shame."

"I know, love," Dad said. "But these things happen, there's no accountin' for the way things go."

"I'll bundle it up and throw it in the dustbin," Mam said.

"No need for that, love, I know what to do with it."

* * *

That year, once again, we, the kids of Mayflower Road, had the grandest bonfire in all the district, and to celebrate this annual and boisterous occasion, Mam produced an enormous tray of treacle toffee, and gave me the job of making sure everyone received a fair share.

What a night it was. Whizzers, bangers and rockets flashed and zoomed and hot roast potatoes were consumed; while high above us, engulfed in flames, sat the best and most expensively dressed Guy Fawkes that Dad had ever made.

Adolf's Spy

Before the birth of television and high-rise flats, living as we did, close to a canal was an integral part of a unique upbringing that nurtured a variety of experiences, never to be forgotten. The excitement of play, the trauma of death, the joy of freedom, and on this odd occasion, the drama of war.

In the year of 1940, while the war raged around us, we, the kids of Mayflower Road, schooled, played and changed our ways not one iota. On winter days, if it was cold enough, the canal became our ice-rink. On summer days, in the heat of the sun, the canal became our swimming pool. And this was one of those days.

The sun was high and strong and the irresistible deep, dark coolness of our canal, drew us like a magnet to its murky depths.

When me and my big brother Colin reached Elston Bridge the place was alive with white, goose-pimpled, naked bodies. Close by the bridge and opposite Walton's foundry, a line of moored canal boats had already become roosting places for a horde of shivering, dripping swimmers. The sound of laughter, splashing, shouting and bragging was all around us.

"I dare thi to dive off yon bridge."

It was Sandy Robson. He was as old as me, but bigger and stronger, and a better swimmer. And he knew it.

Elston Bridge wasn't high, but to dive from it was extremely dangerous. Below the bridge was a watery scrapyard. Rusting bikes and prams and bedsteads and any unwanted sinkable thing was down there, waiting to bruise, impale, or trap any reckless diver.

"I will if thy does," my brother said.

"Don't be daft, Colin," I said. "Tha'll break thi bloody neck."

Undaunted, our Colin ignored me. "C'mon, Robson, thee go first and I'll follow."

I climbed the steps behind them. Bodies parted as the two contestants pushed their way through. The word had spread like wildfire. Everybody had jumped off the bridge, but to dive from it was the next thing to committing hara-kiri. Sandy climbed through the wooden rails and stood poised on the edge. He looked around, grinned and dived without hesitation into the murky depths below. Surfacing almost immediately, he began to tread water and shouting up to us in a taunting voice.

"C'mon, Colin. Are tha scared o' what?"

My brother, not to be outdone, did his dive and surfaced beside him, gasping, grinning and blowing foul water.

I ran down to the towpath and helped them onto the bank.

"How about from the top rail?" Sandy said.

"Suits me," our Colin said. "I'm game if thy is."

Getting a bit fed up of being just a witness I stayed on the towpath.

Once again our Colin and Sandy were the focus of attention. I shaded my eyes against the glare of the sun as Sandy, once again, brimming with confidence, dived with Tarzan-like grace from the top rail and entered the water like a spear.

I held my breath, as Colin, with obvious nervousness, climbed onto the rail. Just at this moment two lads on a makeshift raft made from oil drums floated slowly under the bridge. Our Colin, seeing them, teetered like a drunken man, found his balance and launched himself. His style was loose. His dive was wrong. He hit the canal with a loud, ominous splash, just missing the two would-be sailors. Sandy, still treading water and obviously pleased with himself, shouted:

"That weren't much soddin' good, was it?"

We waited for Colin to surface. Nothing happened. I looked up and down, searching for his face among the many swimmers. No Colin.

"He's havin' us on," Sandy said. But his smile was false, frozen on his face. After what seemed forever I began to panic.

"He's in trouble, Sandy, somethin's up. Go down for him. Please, Sandy, 'urry up!"

Just then, up popped our Colin, just like a cork, spluttering, coughing and blinking; hair plastered to his head like a black skullcap.

"I thought you'd had it, kid." I shouted.

He swam towards me and held out his hand.

"Give us a hand-up, Eric."

As I pulled him out, Sandy gave us a wave and swam off to one of the canal boats.

"I thought you'd had it, kid." I said again.

"There's summat funny down there, Eric."

"Bloody hell, Colin, what is it, a body?"

"No it's not and stop bloody swearing."

"You swear, so why can't I?"

"I'm older than you, so shut up."

"What is it, then? What's down there?"

"It looks like a parcel in a pram."

"A parcel? What's wrong wi' that? There's all sorts in't cut."

"When I went down I caught mi shins on this pram, then I saw it . . . this oilskin parcel lying in the pram . . . I think there's summat in it."

"Why didn't tha bring it up, then?"

"What, and let Sandy Robson an' all flamin' lot o' them see what it is? Not soddin' likely."

"But it might be nowt at all."

"We'll soon find out, give us thi vest."

"You what?"

"Give us thi vest I said."

"What for?"

"Never mind. Give us thi vest. C'mon!"

I gave Colin the vest and squatted down at the canal's edge.

"Now listen to me." Colin said. "Don't panic if I don't come up straight away. I've got to find that soddin' pram again. Alright?"

"I'll not, but mind thisel though, don't get trapped."

"I'll be okay, and if any bugger comes near tell 'em to bugger off."

"But you told me not to swear."

"I'll not be able to hear thi down theer, will I? You daft sod."

And with a swift look around, he cocked up his backside and vanished from sight. I watched the bubbles and ripples he'd left in his wake and said a silent prayer.

Before I'd had the honour of cursing anybody he reappeared clutching my now soggy and bulky vest.

"Here, kid," he gasped, "grab this."

I took the vest and pulled him onto the bank.

"C'mon," he said, "let's get our togs and get back home."

Leaving the bedlam behind, we crossed Elston Bridge and hurried past the narrow footpath which led to the rear entrance of Walton's Foundry. As a precautionary wartime measure against any attack from the canal, the Ministry had erected two massive concrete blocks and a sentry-box which was manned by the Home Guard. Anyone wanting to use the path had to produce an identity card or some other form of identification. Halfway across Gambler's Field the suspense became unbearable.

"C'mon Colin," I said, "let's have a look what it is."

We stopped and sat facing each other in the lush grass. Slowly and with great deliberation, Colin unrolled my dripping vest to reveal a black oilskin bag tied with string. Finally, after a dual effort the knot came free. In what seemed to me like slow motion, Colin opened the bag. The suspense was over. Before us, glinting dully in the afternoon sun was the reason for our hurried departure from the canal. It was a gun.

"Bloody hell!" Colin said. "Bloody hell!"

"It's a gun." I said.

"How can you tell?" Colin said.

He could be a right sarcastic sod, our Colin sometimes.

"Let's get it home, Eric, before somebody comes."

When we reached home Mam was out. Dad, with some reluctance, put aside his cowboy book and listened to our story. He picked up the gun carefully.

"Have you been playing with this?"

"No Dad." We chorused.

"Supposin' it's loaded, eh? One of you could have been killed, you silly sods."

"We didn't, Dad. Honest." I said.

He examined the gun with great care and rubbed his chin.

"By 'eck, it's a German Lugar."

"How did it come to be in the pram, Dad?" I said.

"By chance, probably. Somebody must have thrown it from Elston Bridge."

"Is there any bullets in it?" I said.

"Lucky for you, no."

"Why chuck away an empty gun?"

"'Cos a gun's no use wi' no bullets, that's why." Colin said.

"Could there be a German livin' near us, Dad?" I said.

Dad laughed: "A German? Round here? I doubt it, lad."

Dad ignoring us both gave the gun a good cleaning and wrapped it in one of Mam's dusters.

"Here," he said, "take it to the police station, hand it in and tell them everything you've told me."

Our Colin took the pistol and gave me a sharp dig in the ribs.

"Okay, Dad. Right, Eric, let's be off."

"By the way, lads," Dad said, "you'd better get rid of that vest, tell your Mam some sod pinched it while you were swimmin'."

Out on the street our Colin grabbed me by the arm.

"Listen, Eric, you might be right in what you said."

"What about?"

"About a German getting rid o' that Luger. After all, who else would want to get shut, eh? You tell me."

"I think you're right," I said. "Anybody else would hand it in to the police . . . just like us."

"But we're not handin' it in, Eric."

"We're not?"

"No, Eric, we're not. I've been doin' some thinkin' about this lot."

"What kind o' thinkin'?"

"Supposin' this, Eric, supposin' there is a German, a German spy and he's on one of them canal boats?"

"What would he be doin' on one o' them, Colin?"

"Tell me, Eric, where is those boats moored, eh?"

"Near Elston Bridge, why?"

"An' what's near the bridge, Eric, eh?"

"Walton's Foundry. Everybody knows that."

"That's it, Eric. Walton's Foundry. An iron foundry. A place where stuff's made to help beat the Germans."

"So?"

"Soddin' hell, Eric, do I have to explain every little detail?"

"Do you think the Germans are spying on Walton's then, is that it?"

"Now you're usin' your noggin, kid."

"But why should he have an empty gun?"

"Bloody hell, Eric, I don't know everything . . . Nobody does."

"I was only askin'."

"Anyway, he doesn't need one if he's only sending messages . . . He could send some sort o' signal, disappear and the place could be bombed . . . Who knows?"

"Shall we tell the police, Colin?"

"Not likely, not till we've got some proof."

"What's your plan, then?"

"Right . . . We keep the Luger, then tonight we'll do a bit o' spyin' of our own. Are you with me?"

"If you say so, Colin."

We wandered around for a while then returned home. We went down the entry, into the yard and through the back door. Shouting that we had arrived back, we climbed the stairs to our bedroom. Colin put the automatic under his pillow and began to outline his plan.

After our parents had gone to sleep we would get dressed, slip quietly downstairs, let ourselves out and make our way to the canal bank. From this point the plan became a little hazy, so my brother decided wisely to leave the finer details unsaid.

Anyhow, sleep overcame my enthusiasm, and it would have remained so but for our Colin's rough shaking.

"Waken up, you lazy sod, it's time to get goin'."

Grabbing the pistol, he led the way down our creaky stairs, out into the backyard, up the entry and onto the blacked-out street. Guided by the light of a full moon, we ran across Gambler's Field, past Calman's bone works and along the canal towpath. As we approached Walton's Foundry I gave my brother a nudge.

"What about the guard? How are we goin' to get past?"

"Let's hope he's inside havin' a cuppa." Colin said.

But it wasn't to be. The glow of a cigarette-end from the shadow of the sentry-box told us different.

"What're we goin' to do now?" I said.

We sat by the canal whispering and breathless with excitement.

"I don't know."

"Let's go home, we'll never get past him."

"Just a minute," Colin said. "What's that?"

We peered into the canal. A few yards along we could see a makeshift raft rocking gently and tapping against the brickwork.

"Just the thing." Colin said. "C'mon, kid, and keep quiet."

We climbed aboard the drums, lay belly-down and using our hands as paddles, propelled our way across the water. On reaching the opposite side we hugged the canal bank, floated past the sentinel, under Elston Bridge and came to a stop a few yards short of the first craft. We tiptoed across the towpath and went down into Three Corner Meadow.

"What do we do now?" I whispered.

"Look for somebody signalling, you daft sod."

I knelt in the grass and gazed intently at the shadowy outline of boats. Not a glimmer. I began to get restless.

"Who will they be signalling?" I said.

"Bloody Germans. Who do you think?"

"But where will the Germans be?"

"How the 'eck do I know. You ask some stupid questions, you do."

We fell silent again. The call of a bat echoed thinly through the moonlit night.

"We'll have to get closer." Colin said. "Let's move further up."

We crept up the incline, waited a few minutes, then keeping to the grass, moved slowly along the edge of the towpath. By this time my heart was racing and pounding against my ribs. Suddenly, Colin, who was in front as usual, came to a stop and held up his hand. He pointed a forefinger to indicate the nearest boat. I held my breath and listened. There was no sound, but a chink in a curtain showed us a glimmer of light from within. Once again we went into our tiptoe routine. With heads close together we looked inside. Seated at a table was a British soldier playing some kind of card game, we watched for a while, then Colin gave my sleeve a tug.

"Let's get the name of the boat," he whispered, "and make tracks."

With nervous glances over our shoulder we made our way back to the raft.

"What's an army bloke doin' on a canal boat, kid?" I said.

"I don't know for sure, but supposin' he's one of Adolf's spies, dressed as a British soldier, eh? What about that?"

"And passin' on information about Walton's, is that what you mean, Colin?"

"Bloody hell!"

"What 'ave I said now, Colin? Have I said summat wrong?"

"The soddin' raft it's floated across t'other side."

"Bloody hell!"

"Shut up swearin' an' let's get movin'."

"What are we going to do now, kid?"

"One of two things. Cross over the bridge an' risk bein' caught, or go further along and swim across. What do you think's best?"

"What, an' freeze mi bloody bollocks off. Not likely."

"Keep quiet then."

With the bridge behind us and the gentle lapping of water in our ears we crept slowly and nearer to the sentry-box. There was no one on guard. We walked on confident and relieved.

"Halt! . . . Who goes there?"

I nearly shit myself and froze to the spot. Colin did likewise. The voice cut through the semi-darkness again. Loud. Commanding.

"Who goes there?"

I wanted to shout friend, but the word wouldn't come. We turned round, hands above our heads and walked back to the shadowy challenger. Two feet from him, he shouted again.

"Stop! Declare yourselves."

I noticed that his rifle was pointing straight at our Colin and all of a sudden this wild idea came from nowhere and made me feel better. If he shot our Colin I would have time to escape and run home for Dad.

"We're Colin and Eric." Our Colin said.

"What you doing down here this time of night, eh?"

"We've been lookin' for somebody."

"Oh, aye, and who would that be, then?"

"A German spy." Colin said.

There was a long pause. Then a chuckle.

"A German spy? Round here? . . . Have you gone barmy?"

"He sounds just like Dad", I thought.

"I think we've found him," Colin said.

He took the Luger from his waistband and held it out.

"And we think this is his gun."

"It's not loaded," I said.

The guard hesitated, lowered his rifle and took the pistol.

"You'd better come with me to the gatehouse."

He led us down the narrow, high fenced path to Walton's foundry. The gatehouse was a small brick building protected by sandbags. The room was almost bare. A tall cupboard, a desk and telephone, three battered chairs and a small gas stove with a large, steaming, iron kettle, were its only contents.

He placed two of the chairs together and ordered us to sit. He picked up the telephone and dialled a number.

"Can I speak to Sergeant Colby, please? . . . Oh, it's you sergeant . . . This is Bert Wilton speaking, I'm doing guard duty down at Walton's, I wonder if you can come down straight away, there's a bit of a problem . . ."

A faint voice crackled over the line, to which the guard answered:

"I don't know much about it sergeant, but there's two young lads here with a German Luger; it would be better if you could come down . . . Twenty minutes? Okay, see you then."

Our captor perched his tall, lean frame on the edge of the desk and stared glumly into space. The wait seemed an eternity. The silence almost unbearable. At last, Sergeant Colby made an appearance. Everything about him exuded authority. Body size. Tone of voice and bearing.

Seated behind the desk and facing the three of us, he said:

"Well, Bert, what's all this about, hmm?"

"Right, lads, fire away, tell Sergeant Colby what you told me."

With quite a few promptings from the policeman, Colin and me told our story. While we were talking he picked up the pistol and examined it. After we had finished, he said:

"Who cleaned the gun?"

"Our Dad." Colin said.

"And you're sure about this soldier?"

"Positive." Colin said. "He's on a boat called, Zeus." A few questions later, the policeman got to his feet.

"I don't know what to make of all this, not yet anyway, but there's nothing else you can do now . . . Come on, I'll take you both home."

"Er, you don't need to, er, sir," our Colin said. "We'll manage okay, thank you very much."

"As you will. Anyway, I'll keep you informed of any developments, you can be sure of that."

Dawn was just breaking when my brother and me climbed exhausted into bed and without a word fell fast asleep.

The end result of our wartime adventure came to a rapid, but colourless conclusion, or so we thought. Sergeant Colby kept his word and came personally to inform us of his investigations. Our German agent, it seemed, was a British army deserter. He'd gone AWOL six months previous and had been on the run ever since.

The sergeant, to save us from parental discipline, informed Mam and Dad that because of our persistent efforts, a letter of commendation from London's War Office, was a sure thing. And Mam and Dad, expecting magnificent praises from no other than Winston Churchill himself, did us proud and gave us anything — well, almost anything — we asked for.

We did get a letter. A well written one, full of gratitude . . . Approval . . . Admiration, the lot. It was a great piece of writing; but it hadn't come from Winston. Sergeant Colby, apart from being a good cop and a humanitarian, was also a good man with a pen.

* * *

But it wasn't over. About 6 weeks after our spy-hunting episode, just two hundred yards from Elston Bridge, the bloated body of an unknown man rose to the surface. The blue-serge suit he wore was scrupulously examined. Pockets were turned out and linings checked for maker or vendor. Nothing was found, not even an handkerchief. His shoes too, when scrutinised, also revealed nothing. The man's identity was a complete mystery.

However, when the body was taken to the mortuary and stripped, an astonishing discovery was made. Around his neck, tattooed for perpetuity, was an indelible necklace of minute German swastikas.

Captain Pegleg's Buried Treasure

Some people truly believe that the misfortunes of life comes in threes, and in the case of Jack Pegleg this popular notion proved to be correct. Within minutes of his wife's sudden death the outbreak of World War Two was declared, and Pegleg, in what could only be described as a state of shock, decided there and then to permanently moor his motorised canal barge.

Three days later, after a dignified post-funeral get together with a few canal friends, he returned to the only home he had known for the last 30 years, his beloved boat.

The boat, a legacy left by his wife's only brother, had been the means of escape from the rigours of Mayflower Road. Not many at their age got the chance to break free from the bonds of a rented hovel, to go on and make new friends and create a far deeper and loving relationship that only ended with his wife's untimely death.

Now, to overcome his grief he polished brasses, painted his boat and black-tarred his wooden leg. Chore after chore fell to his methodical, slow consuming ways, until, finally, there was nothing left to do. Except for the occasional visitor and his battered radio, Pegleg's world was a silent one and that winter, marooned by heavy falls of snow, he became tense and morose.

Spring arrived. The war rumbled on, stretching its wicked, bloody trail across the continents. Jack, just like the rest of England, listened daily to every bulletin. Sometimes, in a bid to cleanse himself of war and sloth, he would leave his vessel, pass by derelict allotments and onwards into the countryside until tiredness forced him back to his floating home. And so it went, until one day, out of the chaos of time and unpredictable events, there arrived at Jack's barge, a bowler-hatted, pin-striped town official. That small, dapper visitor brought to Jack some glimmer of hope, some feeling of furfilment to an otherwise dull and meaningless life. For inside one month of that visit, Jack Pegleg, ex-bargee, was responding to Winston Churchill's directive and digging for victory.

Soon, every allotment echoed industriously to the muscular efforts of local people, all intent on sowing and growing, and doing their bit for King and country.

For Jack, this was a time of great change, followed by diligent satisfaction. The situation was ideal, with home and workplace in close proximity, Pegleg was happy; but even the happiest of people sometimes suffer from some indefinable emptiness. Since the death of his wife, Jack had suffered fits of depression and became a trifle cantankerous, and not even the intended camaraderie of his new-found fellow-men could break down the barrier. Even so, the work, the challenge to produce foodstuff, was for him an invigorating experience, and the friendly jibes about a one-legged spud grower could in no way dampen his enthusiasm. Everyone seemed content in their little havens of escape, until, one afternoon, Clem Tatton, Pegleg's next door neighbour, paid him a visit.

"How's life treatin' thi, Jack?" he asked as an opener.

"So, so, Clem," Pegleg replied. "Can't grumble."

"Tell me, Jack, have you had any nocturnal visitors on your place?"

"Perhaps the odd rat or two, why?"

"Some thievin' sod's bin helpin' isel to my belongings, that's why."

"Such as?" Pegleg asked.

"A few spuds . . . the odd cabbage, that sort o' thing."

"Hmm, there's no vegetarian rats round here, Clem, owt else missin'?"

"Nowt, they've not bothered wi' mi tools, just the edible stuff."

"Somebody's makin' their rations stretch out." Jack said.

"We've bin thinkin', me an' the rest," Clem said. "Seein' as your boat's close by, could you do a spot o' police work for us?"

"At night, you mean?"

"If you don't mind."

"Aye, I'll give it a shot, who knows it could be me next."

"That's just what we were thinkin'," Clem said.

"I can't promise it'll be every night, mind."

"That's fair enough. At least summats bein' done."

* * *

A week passed and Pegleg began to doubt Clem Tatton's suspicions and came to the decision that this particular night would be his last. He'd had enough of these nightly vigils, it was time for someone else to take a turn. With his mind made up, he perched on the cabin's roof, wooden leg angled outwards like the shaft of a wheelbarrow and stoked his worn clay pipe. A moon, hindered by scudding clouds lighted and dimmed sky and earth at varying intervals. An hour later, feeling the need of a brew, Jack slid to the deck.

Just at that moment a flash of light from the black of Clem's land caught his wary eye. In the interval of darkness that followed Pegleg could track the bobbing beam as its owner moved at random.

Jack began to plan his next move. There was only one way the intruder could go and that was along the narrow pathway which ran in a dip between the canal towpath and the allotment gardens. If the burglar went the opposite way towards Walton's foundry he would be challenged by the Home Guard. But what could he, a one-legged has-been do to stop some brawny, determined criminal? It was too late to fetch a bobby, or the Home Guard, for that matter. Without really considering the consequences, Pegleg left the confines of his boat and made his tentative way towards the allotments. As he drew level with Clem's place he came to a halt and sat on the grassy slope leading to the bottom pathway. A few minutes later the thud of a falling object followed by someone scrambling over the fence drew his attention. A pause, a grunt of exertion, then the eerie form of the thief drew closer.

"Got what you want?" Pegleg said in a loud voice.

"Bloody hell, you scared mi rotten." The voice was boyish, lacking in depth.

Pegleg still unsure, raised his tone:

"Who are you, what you playin' at, eh?"

"Mi name's Ronnie, Ronnie Wilmot. Who are you anyway?"

A shift of the clouds revealed Ronnie to be about twelve years old, wiry and fairly tall.

"Never mind me," Pegleg said, sliding down the bank.

"What's in the bag?"

"Nowt to do wi' thee, mister."

Then he noticed Jack's wooden leg.

"You're Captain Pegleg, you live on a boat."

"And where do you live, young whippersnapper?"

"Nowt to do wi' thee."

"Don't cheek me young man. C'mon you'd better come with me."

"Where to? What fer?"

"Just come along, you'll come to no harm." Jack said.

"I don't need to . . . I could just run off . . . You'd never catch mi, not wi' a wooden leg you wouldn't."

"I know your name, I'd find you."

"Suppose it's not mi real name, eh?"

"I'd still find you," Jack said. "C'mon, let's go."

The lad, intrigued by his captor's deformity and his local seafaring title, submitted to Jack's bidding and trailed him back to the boat. Once aboard and below deck, Jack made them both a drink.

"Now, Ronnie," he said. "It is your real name isn't it, what's in the bag? Own up and I'll let you go."

Ronnie, somewhat intimidated by Jack's authoritative tone and the claustrophobic surroundings, stayed silent.

"You've been helpin' yoursel' to Clem's veg, haven't you? C'mon own up."

"Who's Clem?"

"A friend o' mine, and that lot belongs to him."

"He's got plenty, it's not like he's short."

"That's beside the point, you're breakin' the law, it s stealing."

"You're goin' to report mi, aren't tha?"

"Not if you make this the last time, I'll not, no."

"If mi Mam finds out she'll kill mi."

"And where does your Mam think this lot comes from?"

"She thinks I'm workin' for it."

"You mean for us on the allotments?"

"Aye."

"And what about your Dad, what does he think, eh?

"Mi Dad's dead, he got killed at Dunkirk."

"Hell, I'm sorry, I didn't know."

"You weren't to know, mister . . . That's why I pinch this lot."

"I don't know what you mean," Pegleg said.

"It's for mi Mam, she's a bit poorly, doctor says she needs plenty o' vitamins and such."

"She's took it bad then?"

"Aye, but she's still workin'."

"Where does she work?"

"Munitions factory. It helps her to forget and get her own back, I suppose."

"I see, and what about your grandparents?"

"There's only mi grandma, I stop wi' her while things are like they are,"

Pegleg, still suffering from the after effects of bereavement felt a deep surge of sympathy for the troubled family.

"Right, Ronnie." He said with a smile. "Pick up your ill-gotten gains and get off home before your grandma misses you."

Ronnie, obviously relieved laughed out loud:

"No chance o' that Captain, I always wait 'til she's snorin' her head off."

"Now listen here, Ronnie." Jack said. "I don't want any more of this thievin'."

"But what about me Mam? We don't get enough rations do her any good."

"Don't worry about that, next time you want anything just ask me."

"But we've no money."

"Do as I say, just ask."

"Thanks Captain."

"C'mon, I'll see you home."

"No need, Mr Pegleg, I've got mi torch, I'll be okay."

"Alright then, but keep a lookout for the air-raid warden."

* * *

So with each passing visit the bond between man and boy nurtured and grew stronger. Pegleg's friends too, knowing of the lad's plight, gave, and asked of nothing in return; but Ronnie being of sound character, paid his dues by working the land with them, and this earned their respect.

One Saturday however, Ronnie failed to turn up; but Pegleg, knowing of the boy's penchant for the silver screen smiled to himself and thought no more of it. The following day, Ronnie made an appearance.

"Now, lad," Pegleg said. "Did tha enjoy tha rest?"

"They've taken mi Mam away, Mr Pegleg, she's proper poorly this time."

"It's perhaps for the best, lad, and a visit from you will cheer her no end."

"They've taken her a good way away, Mr Pegleg."

"Oh, I see, don't worry they know what they're doin' these doctors."

"Can I come and live wi' you on the boat?"

This sudden, straight question left Jack flummoxed and silent.

"Can I?"

"What about your grandma, Ronnie? She'll need you more than ever now."

"I don't care I want to stay wi' you near the allotments."

"Do you think that's fair?"

"I'll see her, I'll take her some veg regular like, I'll keep me eye on her."

Pegleg caught up in a quandary of emotions and confusing thoughts decided against making any immediate decision.

"We'll see, lad, we'll see. Now c'mon and let's get some diggin' done."

* * *

A couple of nights later, Pegleg suffering the effects of an exceptionally warm climate and feeling the need of some liquid socialising, passed through the welcoming portals of the Three Crowns Inn. That very same night a raging storm unleashed its terrible strength and fury to play havoc and mayhem with its earthbound mortals.

High winds blew, stinging rains lashed, thunder rumbled and lightning cracked and streaked across the heavens, and chose its victims with unerring precision. So wrathful were the elements that the good landlord, hospitable to a fault, locked his doors and imprisoned his customers, making everyone, including himself, happy recipients of ale and profit. On the stroke of midnight the storm abated, the doors were thrown open and a happy band of imbibers poured out into the rain drenched street. Pegleg, more unsteady than usual, left his companions and made his way home, Picking his way by torchlight he peered through the early morning gloom. Another few yards and he would be home. He wrinkled his nose. Was that the smell of burning? Surely not. Not out here, not at this hour, not after all that rain. He stopped dead in his tracks. God! His home, what he could see of it, was a smouldering wreck.

"God in Heaven!" cried Pegleg. "Who would do such a thing?"

Then like an arrow to its mark the realisation of this devastation struck through his anguish.

"Damn!" he shouted to the darkness. "The lightning! the damn lightning!"

Standing alone at the water's edge he did the only thing humanly possible. He cursed and ranted and raved until his venom was spent. Finally, through the numbness of defeat he began to collect his thoughts. He fumbled in his pockets and found amongst loose change, three keys held together by a piece of string. Thank God! One was for the cabin of his boat, the other two for the allotment door and a shed where he stored his tools.

"At least I can get mi head down," he said to himself.

The next few days convinced Jack Pegleg that true friendship was indeed something to be cherished.

A few modifications to his shed, a bed from Clem and other donations from the rest and Pegleg settled into his new home. With accommodation assured, Pegleg turned his attention to the wreck of his boat. After collecting some sentimental items, one of his boatmen pals towed the stricken craft to the nearest boatyard, with the understanding that it should be dismantled and that the engine and anything else of value should go to the boat builder as payment for work done.

One day, a troubled Ronnie began to ask Pegleg some searching questions.

"Do you like livin' on your own, Captain?"

"Not really, lad, but I'm gettin' used to it."

"Why don't you come an' live wi' me and grandma?"

Jack laughed, "I don't think your grandma'd appreciate an owd codger like me under her feet."

"Aye she would, I've asked her."

"You shouldna done that, lad, the poor woman's got enough on her plate."

"She doesn't mind."

"I'm sorry lad, but I'd rather be on mi own."

"She'll give you your dinner an' everythin'."

"I'll be alright, I'll manage. Tell her thanks anyway."

Ronnie, not to be completely thwarted, set in motion alternative arrangements. With himself acting as conveyor, food was transported back and forth at convenient intervals. Root vegetables he took to his grandma and cooked meals he returned to Jack, who, thankful for any well prepared, sustaining food, reheated them on his primus stove and did them justice.

One Saturday morning, after a strenuous session of digging, weeding and planting, Jack became uncommonly breathless, this and a sharp chest pain forced him indoors to rest. Ronnie, concerned for his well-being, went with him, made him a cup of tea and asked did he want a doctor.

"No, lad, no. What would a doctor do wi' an owd wreck like me?"

In an effort to put his friend at ease, Ronnie said

"How did you lose your leg, Captain?"

"Down the pit, lad. I was only a sprat at the time, but it put the kibosh on me being a miner, but I never regretted it, not for one minute."

"Why do you paint it?"

Pegleg smiled. "To keep the woodlice away . . . no I'm jokin' it helps to preserve it." His smile broadened. "To preserve it for thee."

"For me?"

"Aye, when I pass on it's yours, lad."

"An' what would I do wi' a wooden leg?"

"You'd be surprised, young feller, there's always summat tha can do wi' a second-hand wooden leg."

139

"I can't think of anything," Ronnie said. "Anyway, what you goin' on about? You're not goin' to die, not fer a long time yet, so don't be daft."

* * *

One week to the day later, Ronnie, prompt as usual, arrived at the allotment to do an hours work and to inform Pegleg of his mother's welcome return, after which, a visit to the pictures would make his weekend complete and satisfying.

However, he was met on the canal bank by Clem, who, trying his best to sound unconcerned, informed Ronnie that Pegleg had been rushed to hospital with severe chest pains. The boy, having witnessed one attack decided to pay him a visit. When he arrived at the infirmary the receptionist gave him a searching glance and asked for his name.

"Ronnie Wilmot," Ronnie answered. "Why, what's wrong?"

The receptionist picked up a phone.

"Just a moment," she said and spoke into the receiver.

"Ronnie Wilmot's here . . . he's only a lad . . . alright, I'll tell him."

She replaced the receiver and turning to Ronnie said:

"There's a nurse coming to see you, she won't be long."

A few minutes later a pretty uniformed young woman arrived and introduced herself as Nurse Milly.

"I'm afraid it's bad news, Ronald," she said. "Your friend Jack has died, before he passed away he told me all about you."

"He can't be dead, missus, not Pegleg, he can't be."

"I regret to say, he is, Ronald. Before he died he asked me to give you something."

She motioned to the receptionist, who on bending down behind the counter produced Pegleg's wooden leg.

"He wanted you to have it, Ronald," the nurse said, "and he asked me to give you this message. He said to tell you to look under the cushion where he rested the stump of his leg, and that you will find a letter there."

The nurse gave Ronnie the wooden leg and patted his head affectionately.

"Bye, Ronald, and never forget, that old man loved you like a son."

It had been some time since Ronnie had shed tears, not even his father's death had done that. To him his father had died a hero fighting a war against the enemy, and because of this his proudness had overcome his grief. But somehow, Pegleg's death was different. He had replaced his missing parent. He had been someone to look up to, to take advice from. Someone to share his inner thoughts with, and because of these things, Ronnie was going to miss him, and he sobbed bitterly.

After braving some curious looks of astonishment, Ronnie finally arrived at the allotment and entered Pegleg's shed. Once settled, Ronnie removed the soiled and well-worn cushion from its rest to reveal a brown envelope with his name on it. He opened it, drew forth a sheet of paper and began to read.

"Dear Ronnie. It had to happen one day and that is why you are reading this. As regards to my funeral, Clem Tatton has all the details and a sufficient sum to see to my rest. Over these past few months you and me have become like father and son, well, grandfather and grandson, the point being lad, you've made my last days happy ones, and I thank you for them. To show you my appreciation, take a spade, go to the east side of the allotment, by the end of the third lettuce drill, and dig. Down there you'll find a tin box, there's all sorts inside, it's for you and the family. I have just one last request, inside the box you'll find a photograph of me and my wife taken on the boat a good few years ago. Would you give us an home, lad and stick us over your mantelpiece, that's the only way Mabel and me will be remembered. That's it Ronnie. Thanks for everything."

* * *

And sure enough, Ronnie dug his hole, found the box, which contained money and jewellery, and of course the photograph, and which Ronnie, true to his friend's last wish, gave it pride of place over the fireplace. And, in a cosy corner, close by the fire, he stood Jack's wooden leg, which he never failed to paint on every anniversary of Jack's demise.

Not Far from Wigan Pier

Born and raised in a rented house, inhaling the stench of Calman's factory, does something to a person. For instance, when asked by strangers the whereabouts of my upbringing, I became devious. I never lied; I just sidestepped a little.

"Not far from Wigan Pier'" I'd say, and change the subject as soon as possible.

Mayflower Road was a cobbled road which came to a stop a few hundred yards from the Leeds to Liverpool canal. Positioned between our cobbled paradise and the canal, stood Calman's bone works, a firm whose produce of bone-meal, glue, and cowhide, was responsible for the unholy stench that was forever present; morning, noon, and night; day after day, year after year.

Actually, the factory was under new management. Jack Calman, the original owner, had worked and worried himself to death, and Owen, his brother, not wanting to go the same way, had sold out to Frazier Pullman, an ex-manager at Calman's who had been sacked by Jack twelve months prior to his demise.

Frazier Pullman, not wanting to lose the power of a reputable trading name, decided to keep the name of Calman for all his buying and selling transactions. But Frazier, a man of dubious principles, put his stamp of authority on other things. New machinery was installed. A longer working day was put into practice. Union rules, and rights of the individual were waived. And disciplinary action against anyone who interrupted company policies, was severe and final.

* * *

Our house was the last one in Mayflower Road, and consequently, the one nearest Calman's factory. Dad, like many more local residents, had worked for Jack Calman for many years. Unpleasant though it was, work of any kind in 1936 was more than welcome. At sixteen, I was still unemployed, fast losing hope, and always broke. To help eke out Dad's meagre wages and to overcome the many wants of me and my brother, Toby, Mam took in washing. It was a grim existence. There was no escape, or any remote possibility of improving our living standards. But the drudgery, the stench, and the unseemly environment, didn't disturb or affect us. We were part of it. We had never known anything else. To compromise for these adverse conditions, we had the camaraderie of friends and neighbours. Neighbours who, in time of trouble and setbacks, were on hand to help and advise in any way possible.

One day, Dad, in a desperate attempt to get me off the streets (and, of course, to help with the family's economic needs) asked (probably begged) Frazier Pullman to give me a job. And much to Dad's astonishment, he agreed to give me a three month trial.

My first day was easy. The "bone crusher" as it was called, was housed in an isolated building nicknamed the "bone shop". The operator, George Benbow, a neighbour and life long friend of Dad's, fed animal bones into the crusher. It then came out at the other end as bone-meal fertiliser. It was my job to keep George supplied with enough bones to keep him and the machine busy, and to spade the finished product into sacks, ready for the warehouse. As simple as that.

* * *

It was almost three o'clock and I was looking forward to our fifteen minute respite; but it never came. The next few minutes became a traumatic blur of shock, time, and motion. A spine-chilling scream from George. His limp body slumped grotesquely against the machine. His right arm somewhere inside. His final moans and curses before collapsing. The red stop button. The dash to Pullman's office. The confusion. The frantic phone calls . . . and the ambulance. I will never forget that day for as long as I live.

Dad took George's accident badly, and for the umpteenth time that night, he thumped the arm of his chair and swore.

"I always said George was a damn fool."

Mam sighed wearily.

"There's no need to keep on and on. It's 'appened and it can't be undone . . . it's over and done with."

Dad was adamant.

"Oh no it's not, not by a long chalk, not if it's owt to do wi' me."

"And what can you do, eh? Just what can you do?"

"You'll see," Dad said ominously.

"You won't be doing George any favours, that's for sure," Mam said.

"No, but suppose it 'appens again? Suppose Pullman decides to put our Eric in George's place, eh?"

Mam looked at me and frowned. Dad's assumptions had got her worried.

"Don't talk daft. He won't do that. Eric's new to the job. Besides, he's too young . . . isn't he?"

"You're missing the point, woman . . . somebody . . . anybody, will be asked . . . nay, forced, to operate that damn mantrap."

"But what can you do, Fred? You're nowt but a labourer."

"I'll do something," Dad said. "Just see if I don't"

All this talk had me baffled.

"Why do you keep on about the machine, Dad, what's wrong wi' it?"

"It has no safety guard, lad, there was never one fitted," Dad said.

"But why?"

"Ask me another," Dad said. "It came from the manufacturers without one, was put into operation and forgotten."

"Why can't one be fitted now," I asked

"Because all Pullman ever thinks about is production and profit. He won't stop that damn machine for nowt nor nobody."

"Can't it be done after hours?"

"Oh, aye . . . and pay a firm overtime rates? He won't do that either."

Before going to bed, Dad had made it abundantly clear that George's accident was going to be Frazier Pullman's downfall.

True to his word, Dad moved in for the kill. By dinner time the following day, he brought the factory's entire production to a standstill. Workmates still reeling from George's accident were in a sympathetic mood. Besides, Pullman's stringent rules of employment were far from being popular. The time was ripe for strike action. A determined push from Dad, and his wish for better and safer working conditions seemed about to be fulfilled. Everybody, except bosses and clerks agreed to down tools. Pullman went berserk. However, three days later, with his rage now under control, his natural cunning surfaced. Knowing the strengths and weaknesses of every employee, he struck. In the confines of his office, each of his chosen victims was given an ultimatum; work or join the dole queue. By Friday the dispute was over. Everyone except Dad and me went back to work. We were sacked.

* * *

Mam never forgave Dad, and for weeks a black depression gripped the four of us. To supplement our inadequate state benefit, Mam, already on the point of exhaustion, took in even more washing. Then, just to make things worse, our Toby fell ill. Doctor Merry diagnosed diptheria, and for a while my young brother was seriously ill. And, but for the assiduous attention of the good doctor, would most certainly have died. Even when out of imminent danger, Doctor Merry wasn't satisfied.

"I've done all I can," he told Mam, "but he has got to rest . . . at least two months in bed, and definitely no walking whatsoever."

"I'll look after him, Doctor," Mam said.

"You both need a rest, Mrs Boyle, somewhere away from here."

He patted Mam's arm and smiled.

"On some tropical island, perhaps."

"The further from the stink of Calman's the better, eh Doc?" Dad said.

* * *

In marriage, Aunt Agnes had fared better than Mam. She had wed a rural man, who managed a farm five miles west of the town. They were a childless couple, but lived contentedly in an ivy smothered cottage close to Uncle Tom's place of work. It had been months since Aunt Agnes's last visit; but on this particular occasion the coming together of the two women was one of sisterly compassion and determination. After their usual exchange of news and gossip, and a peep at our Toby whose bed was downstairs; Aunt Agnes produced from a wicker basket a variety of cooked meats and delicious home-made cakes. And Mam, not to be outdone completely, brought out her best crockery.

"Well Agnes," Mam said between sips of tea, "how did you hear about all this lot, then?"

"Well, it were Fred, he came up to the cottage . . ."

"Oh, aye, he kept that to 'isel' . . . just wait till I see him."

"Now don't be getting on to him, he was only thinking of you and the lad."

"What's he been saying then?"

"He wants you and Toby to come and stay."

"You what?"

"He wants you both up at the cottage, and me and Tom agree."

"Me? I can't go. Who'll look after Eric and his Dad?"

"They'll manage, Helen. Fred's no fool, he'll make sure Eric's alright, won't he, Eric?"

They both looked across the table at me. I took another scone and agreed.

"We'll be alright, Mam, it'll do you and our Toby good to get away. Anyhow, what's a couple of months, it'll fly over."

"Listen," Aunt Agnes said, "from what I can gather Toby still needs a lot of motherly care and attention. Are you going to deny him that? If so, I'll say no more."

There wasn't much else to be said. Aunt Agnes had won the day, and Mam, I'm sure, was glad to be the loser.

The following morning, a pony and trap with Uncle Tom at the reins, arrived at our front door, and in next to no time, our Toby, and Mam, were whisked away in a whirl of wheels and dust.

* * *

Left alone, Dad and me weren't exactly helpless but with a lack of both domestic know-how and Mam's wash day wages, we were soon in trouble. First we received a warning letter about rent arrears. A notice to quit soon followed. Dad went begging to Frazier Pullman, but to no avail. We trudged miles looking for work of any kind but there was none to be had. Another notice to quit dropped through the letterbox. That was when Dad did some serious thinking, and went off to visit Mam and our Toby. The next day, over a kipper dinner, all was revealed.

"I've been up to the cottage, Eric."

"Oh, aye, how's Mam and our Toby then?"

"They're okay, lad, but it was Uncle Tom I went to see really."

"He's not ill, is he?"

"You're going up there, Eric. Uncle Tom's found you work on the farm, and a bed to go wi' it."

"And what about you, Dad? I can't leave you here, not on your own."

"Well, your uncle knows somebody who's on the lookout for a boatman."

"A canal man, you?"

"Aye, an' he reckons the job's mine if I want it."

"And are you takin' it?"

"Money's poor, but there's a bunk where I can get mi head down."

"I don't like it, Dad, we'll be miles apart."

"It's the only way, son, don't worry we'll all be together one day."

* * *

A week later, with the soil of farmland under my nails, I paused for breath and looked across the valley towards the town I'd left. And there, among the smoking stacks and towering mills, I could just make out a winding canal which I knew most certainly ran past Calman's factory, not far from Wigan Pier.

ISIS publish a wide range of books in large print, from fiction to biography. A full list of titles is available free of charge from the address below. Alternatively, contact your local library for details of their collection of ISIS large print books.

Details of ISIS complete and unabridged audio books are also available.

Any suggestions for books you would like to see in large print or audio are always welcome.

7 Centremead
Osney Mead
Oxford OX2 0ES
(01865) 250333